The Avenue
Bearing the Initial
of Christ
into the New World

The Avenue
Bearing the Initial
of Christ
into the New World

Poems 1946–64
by Galway Kinnell

BOSTON

HOUGHTON MIFFLIN COMPANY

Library of Congress Cataloging in Publication Data

Kinnell, Galway, 1927–
The avenue bearing the initial of Christ into the
New World; poems 1946–64.

I. Title.
PS3521.I582A95   811'.5'4   74–1109
ISBN 0–395–18628–5

PRINTED IN THE UNITED STATES OF AMERICA

Certain of the poems in this book have previously
appeared in the following books and magazines:
*The Atlantic Monthly, The Beloit Poetry Journal,
Chelsea, Choice, Epoch, The Hudson Review,
Modern Age, The Nation, The New Orleans Poetry
Journal, New Poems by American Poets, New World
Writing #3, The New Yorker, Noonday, The Paris
Review, Perspective, The Pocket Book of Modern
Verse, Poetry, The Prairie Schooner, The Princeton
University Library Chronicle,* and *Voices.*

v   10 9   8   7   6   5   4

THIS BOOK IS a collection of all the poems from my first eighteen years of writing that I have published in book form. They are from three books: *First Poems 1946–1954,* which came out in a limited edition, and *What a Kingdom It Was* and *Flower Herding on Mount Monadnock,* which have been out of print for several years.

Reading these poems over, I find I have not become at all detached or objective about them, as I had imagined I would. I don't seem to notice their structures, or forms, or metaphors, or any of their character as made objects. They are much more like souvenirs, for as I read through them I remember my life in the time when I wrote them — my emotional and intellectual life, and even more, the persons, events, and places surrounding their composition. I can remember with a clarity that startles me the room in which I set down this poem or that — even a room I might have occupied but a day or two. Luckily — or this would be a very long preface — I feel no promptings to write out the commentary that would correspond to these feelings.

I do need to say a word about the versions that appear here. The poems in *First Poems* are as they were in the original edition; the revisions in those poems I have described in the separate prefatory note. In the case of *What a Kingdom It Was* and *Flower Herding on Mount Monadnock,* many of the poems appear in versions slightly different from those in the original editions. Most of these changes were made while I was reading the poems to audiences. Standing at the podium, just about to say a line, I would feel come over me a definite reluctance to say it as written. Gradually I learned to trust this reluctance. I would either drop the line altogether (discovering the poem did not suffer from the loss but improved on account of it), or else invent on the spot a revision of it. I would write these changes into my copies of the books and use the altered versions in subsequent readings. This is the first time I have entered them into the printed text.

GALWAY KINNELL

Sheffield, Vermont
September, 1973

CONTENTS

First Poems 1946–1954

What a Kingdom It Was

Flower Herding on Mount Monadnock

First Poems 1946-1954

To My Mother

PART I

AUTHOR'S NOTE

I HAVE CHOSEN these poems out of some hundreds I wrote — and mercilessly revised — in my late teens and early twenties.

It might have turned out better for me if, during that period of my life, I had written less and given myself more to silence and waiting. At least those arduous searches for the right iambic beat and the rhyme word seem now like time which could have been better spent. I will never know, and in any event, it is not possible for me to regret a travail which released in me so much energy and excitement, to which I gave myself so entirely, and which saved me. The leftovers, these few pieces of verse, whatever their worth for someone else, I hold in kindly affection.

As I was preparing this collection, Charles G. Bell produced from his files all the first, unrevised versions of my poems — versions which I myself had long since thrown away. I discovered those first versions were almost always superior to the revised ones — which says little for my powers of recognition and revision. The poems in this book, therefore, are mostly in their earliest form, some of them cut considerably, others patched up here and there with lines from the revisions.

It would be ungracious of me to thank Charles Bell for that faithful guardianship, since my debt to him with regard to these poems is so much greater and deeper. Through his own poems, which were to make up his *Songs for a New America,* I had my first glimpses into what poetry could be; and for many years Charles was the only person who gave me a sense that my writings might not be private delusions but actual poems. I still have no better reader or closer friend.

I also want to express a rather belated thanks to the editors of *The Beloit Poetry Journal,* particularly Robert H. Glauber, who published many of my early poems and gave me considerable encouragement.

GALWAY KINNELL

Deyá
March, 1970

3

Acknowledgment is made to the following magazines in which certain of these poems were first published: *The Bard Review, The Beloit Poetry Journal, Nassau Lit, The Nation, New Poems by American Poets* and *The New Mexico Review.* "A Winter Sky" was first published in *The New Yorker.* "The Old Moon" and "The Feast" were first published in *Poetry.*

Two Seasons

1

The stars were wild that summer evening
As on the low lake shore stood you and I
And every time I caught your flashing eye
Or heard your voice discourse on anything
It seemed a star went burning down the sky.

I looked into your heart that dying summer
And found your silent woman's heart grown wild
Whereupon you turned to me and smiled,
Saying you felt afraid but that you were
Weary of being mute and undefiled.

2

I spoke to you that last winter morning
Watching the wind smoke snow across the ice,
Told how the beauty of your spirit, flesh,
And smile had made day break at night and spring
Burst beauty in the wasting winter's place.

You did not answer when I spoke, but stood
As if that wistful part of you, your sorrow,
Were blown about in fitful winds below:
Your eyes replied your worn heart wished it could
Again be white and silent as the snow.

A Walk in the Country

We talked all morning, she said
The day's nice, on this nice summer
Day let's walk where birds glide
At berries ripening everywhere.
And I thought, is it only me such
Beauty refuses to touch?

But I walked all the same, to please
What only an arm held close,
Through a green wood to a space
Where grass was turned over by a farmer whose
Rickety horses ploughed
While crow and robin sang out loud.

She said it was nice. It was.
But I could hear only in the close
Green around me and there in the dark
Brown ground I walked on, meadowlark
Or other thing speak sharp of shortness
That makes us all and under like that grass.

Island of Night

I saw in a dream a beautiful island
Surrounded by an abrasive river,
And soon it was all rubbed into river and
Gone forever, even the sweet millet and the clover.
Then it was night: out of dark caves
Came the thunder of horses — across the black
Desert at the touch of their hooves
Hundreds of colors kept blooming. I awoke
And touched you and your eyes opened
Into the river of darkness around us
And we were together and love happened.
I do not wonder that men should bless
The down-tearing gods, who also let us lift
These islands of night against their downward drift.

The Comfort of Darkness

Darkness swept the earth in my dream,
Cold crowded the streets with its wings,
Cold talons pursued each river and stream
Into the mountains, found out their springs
And drilled the dark world with ice.
An enormous wreck of a bird
Closed on my heart in the darkness
And sank into sleep as it shivered.

Not even the heat of your blood, nor the pure
Light falling endlessly from you, like rain,
Could stay in my memory there
Or comfort me then.
Only the comfort of darkness,
The ice-cold, unfreezable brine,
Could melt the cries into silence,
Your bright hands into mine.

Passion

At the end of a day of walking we found
A hill for our camp, and we ate
By the low fire and sat up to wait
For the stars and the embers. It was not late
When the whisper of our love was the only sound.

Then we were quiet together, like a footfall
A long time vibrant on the pine-needled ground,
Your body touching me, and in the air around
A flute of memory joining the sound
Of your breath and the noise of some small animal.

Overhead the stars stood in their right course.
Later a mourning dove stirred the night
With soft cries. I was deaf, and the light
Out of the east fell on extinguished sight.
My new eyes searched the passion of the stars.

The Feast

Juniper and cedar in the sand,
The lake beyond, here deer-flesh smoking
On the driftwood fire. And we two
Touching each other by the wash of the blue
On the warm sand together lying
As careless as the water on the land.

Now across the water the sunset blooms.
A few pebbles wearing each other
Back into sand speak in the silence;
Or else under the cliff the surf begins,
Telling of another evening, and another,
Beside lapping waters and the small, lapped stones.

The sand turns cold — or the body warms.
If love had not smiled we would never grieve.
But on every earthly place its turning crown
Flashes and fades. We will feast on love again
In the purple light, and rise again and leave
Our two shapes dying in each other's arms.

Told by Seafarers

1

It is told by seafarers
To the children who would go to sea,
When the moon lies full on the sea
It is a time when the life-bearers

Abound in the deep, and a pillar
Of water from the rocking sea
Rises, as the god sea
To the moon is an unerring sailor.

2

Fair girl — and here on the grasses
Of long afternoons, as on a sea-
Floor grasses wave in the still sea,
We lie together, in this grass oasis,

And teach you how the sea rises
Or grass teems in the sea,
When the moon lies full on the sea,
As seafarers tell, in the sea's disguises.

Night Song

I cannot think who is guilty,
One or the other, both — I remember
Only the turning of platters *leaving me*
Blue blue Jezebel — so now I hear

Outside in the raining city
The poor shiver and go on walking and the unfed
Ask alms or shelter and get pity
And I know the lonely are afraid in their beds.

A Winter Sky

Behind our back the golden woods
Held the gold of a great season
As we lay on the shore of the woods
And watched the long afternoon
Dying in golden light in the woods.

Before us the brown marsh
Brought the dark water, dry grass,
Cattails, waste of the close-cropped marsh,
And the hunters' blinds were watching
For traffic on the blinded marsh.

It had been a long, beautiful fall
And as we sat on the shore remembering
The season behind us, the golden fall,
One of us said to the other
There is never an end to fall.

But when two ducks flew away from winter
A gun reached out and caught one
And dropped it like snow in winter,
And without looking back or understanding
The first flew on alone into winter.

We rose as dusky light filled the woods
And looked out over the brown marsh
Where a dog swam and where the fall
Covered the land like a winter
And the sky was empty without cloud or bird.

PART II

Walking Out Alone
in Dead of Winter

Under the snow the secret
Muscles of the underearth
Grow taut
In the pain, the torn love
Of labor. The strange
Dazzled world yearning dumbly
To be born.

Spring Oak

Above the quiet valley and unrippled lake
While woodchucks burrowed new holes, and birds sang,
And radicles began downward and shoots
Committed themselves to the spring
And entered with tiny industrious earthquakes,
A dry-rooted, winter-twisted oak
Revealed itself slowly. And one morning
While the valley underneath was still sleeping
It shook itself and it was all green.

The Gallows

Turmoil finds conclusion
Somewhere. Only the years we spend
Forgetting and learning, courting illusion,
Divorcing old hopes — their promised end
Ends when the heart has formed a fusion
With the head, and the bloody foam is spanned
By reason, resignation; the dark ocean
Where the whales rove lies flat as the sand
Behind us. Turmoil owns such motion
We cannot wish, so fond
Of the torn joy, to fashion
Final peace. Dear is the bond
Bind hearts to desolation.

The cry of the wolf is longing,
Sad is the low sea-moan;
When the head's gallows are hanging
A heart, a youth's cry is pain.

A Walk in Highland Park

We came upon it suddenly — I said,
"Something red is burning in those leaves."
Leaves we would have thought, such shape they had,
The willow's leaves of fall. "That red depraves
The tree, it tells of the permanence of tears,
I think that only what is happy endures."

We turned and ran down through the yellow thorns.
But the wind about my ears played this one tune:
Upon that hill the winterberry burns,
And sorrow's coals are all that will remain.
Though quite a runner when my youth was young,
Now I cannot pace that winter song.

In the Glade at Dusk

I come back obedient:
I hear again in the leaves
My days begin, and in the grave
Light lean my body waiting — for what
If not those vanished flames to make me brave?

But the days of the suffered flame
Forsake me, and the days yet to be endured
Ring me around, and the sun puts its fire
On the trees, and wind blows in the teeth
Of days the last day only shall consume.

The glade catches fire, and where
The birds build nests they brood at evening
On burning limbs. Spirit of the wood, dream
Of all who have ever answered in the glade at dusk —
And grass, grass, blossom through my feet in flames.

The Old Moon

I sat here as a boy
On these winter rocks, watching
The moon-shapes toil through the nights —
I thought then the moon
Only wears her mortality.

Then why to these rocks
Do I keep coming back, why,
The last quarter being nearly
Wasted, does the breath
Come back dragoning the night?

Unless, perhaps,
The soul, too, is such a country,
Made of flesh and light,
And wishes to be whole
And therefore dark.

Sunset at Timberline

I

"I watch this sonovabitch
Buy himself a fifty-cent
Cigar. Dying for the butt
I track him all over town.
When he's smoked it down
To the last inch
He tamps
The fucking thing out
On a lamp-
post and sticks it in his pocket . . ."

"Shit,
Today I see this cat
Blow his nose,
And right in front of the shoeshine
Boys he bends down
And greases his goddam shoes
With his snots . . ."

2

At timberline
A few great, skinless trees
Are clinging, blown almost
Flat,
Like pressed
Flowers. Below me the rainclouds open
To the sunset. In that
Last burst
Of light the window of, perhaps, a flophouse
Flashes.

Primer for the Last Judgment

When Jesus bruised his toe on stone
Men crowned him — all of them,
The pure and the impure — punctured
Finger and toe, and pinned him there,
And coughed less from conscience than
Then called for traditional values, unaw
They were asking their own liquidation.
"The end is at hand," said Paul.
But it did not arrive, that looked-for day
Of devastation, except at its own slow ga
Daily the spent heart came home to find
A space with the dimensions of home
Ambiguously empty like the three-days' to

And now with us: only a few
Years back, at war's close, the sun
Touching the Pacific found
Two cities crumbled. And men
World over asked, "Has the end begun?"
Maybe it has; maybe it shall come
Exploding flesh off the innocent bones,
Mechanized, official, and at once.
Or maybe it has crueler ways —
Dread of the body, the passion to subdue —
Not to be announced until it is done,
Which is each day from this day
Until the last tomb clutches the last bone.

Indian Bread

In childhood, when the ferns came up,
We would gather the roots and stew them in a pot
Letting the sprays lie broken in the grass,
Then dump the mush and bake it in loaves,
Taste it, spit it out, and leave it all for dead,
Some grey puke in the grass, our Indian bread.

Last spring I made the trip back
To the woods where we used to cook
That failed bread. It was overgrown —
Streets, curbs, hydrants, hedges, lawns,
Low-roofed houses where the people burn
Their lives out on the site of the lost fern.

I talked with the owner of a place,
Told him of the old fern-kitchen his house
Was built on. He laughed, said he reckoned
He'd cook himself a few years yet, then find
A new spot, where his kids too could take a pot,
Boil the ferns, taste them, spit them out.

On the way home I looked down
On a last woodland drifting in unbroken green,
I saw moving through it the pre-ghosts of bulldozers.
Dear God, why didn't it ever make,
This wild land where the ferns came up in spring,
For us who wasted it, Indian bread worth eating?

PART III

Conversation at Tea

1

My love had been splendid
For brilliant eyes,
Dancing bodies, star-wheels
Through the night, for flights
Of morning birds, symphonic skies
At noon, all forms of sensual delight,
All willing worlds at once. But the heart mad,
Their tinsel tore. And I declared
My war on every grain God made.

2

War, I would judge, is tragic,
But the difference between
A tragic action on the stage
And off is — one is only mimic.
If you are so insane
As to wish — how do you say? — soul-purge,
By all means go to the theater
But never fight a war.

Come, take two seats at Cyrano
Or better, Evans doing Hamlet
(But what a shame it's cut!)
Or best, the Old Vic
Is bringing Lear here next week.
But then, the theater, it's just too —
Too something — for a man like you.

Why don't you use instead my study
And lose yourself in Chaucer.
Though my classics are a trifle dusty
For you a book is still a book I'm sure.

3

Who is it I am searching for tonight?
What disembodied voice can I surround
With flesh? Like calls of Puck there float
Into my troubled memory the sounds
Of all those voices mingling from the past —
Who is it I am seeking in this waste?

I have mourned with Troilus — not quite in jest
Known the moping madness to declare
His love; and betrayed, called the world a waste
And vanity with heart too deadly sober;
With Sampson too, and Adam, for a love misplaced —
I have mourned with Troilus and the rest.

And swaggering with Cyrano, and travelling
To the moon, and sweeping with a plume
The threshold of the stars, my restless craving
Took bravado for its meat — O spume
Of glory, your vapored kind can only go
With dreams, or swagger there with Cyrano.

And on the heath shall I continue seeking?
Has the storm that lashed us then subsided
Yet, that struggled with the bitter breaking
Of a mind and heart, has it faded
For me yet, or only now begun?
And shall I through the heath continue on?

Who spoke those self-tormentings, were they yours,
Or mine, or Hamlet's own? Whose voice

Is no difference, what head invented
Doesn't matter — the Prince of all of us
Opened the pain of solitude and cursed
The tyrant stars. Do not ask who said them first.

I have been all these hearts, and more,
Heroes, criminals, frauds, and tortured fools,
I have merged my spirit with the fair
And with souls as dark as blood or bowels,
And yet I know more of providence or fate
That who my heart is searching for tonight.

4

Yesterday I saw you
And you did not speak,
You walked as if — allow
Me to be trite —
You walked in a daze.
Do you concentrate
On things so bleak
You cannot see, for thought, your friends?
I know you saw my face
And yet as if our hands
Had never touched, you
Did not know me,
Or even seem to know
Yourself. This struck me strangely,
Your silence, since
Here we are sipping tea
And talking in present tense.
Let's agree, now we are together,
Friendship is forever.

5

I have struck gems in several friends,
Perhaps in more than most, certainly

In more than you, whose delicate tea
Tends more to water. But this is surely
Because the stars rule our destiny
Or God plots out our ends.

My drink is crude and bitter
But at least I made the stuff myself.
You might concede that nature made me better
At hunting diamond mines than you, yet if
You doubt, let me recount the story of
Two friendships now a-tatter.

Chris was one, whose fine fierce spirit spent
Its up-pent fury arguing with me
Who wandered worlds with him. One day he penned
His testament and died. If he could see
Me now, against my heart's depravity,
He could not lift, for tears, his hand.

Another friend was Gib, who did not die,
But wished to change the world, and found
It would not change. His heart fell utterly
To dust, though sometimes still he smiles around
The corners of his mouth. I saw him ruined,
He cannot therefore speak to me.

These friends were fast, for life-long working,
But as you see, a friend is not eternal.
Sometimes walking on the streets, or talking
Over tea, I drowse, conversing with an angel
Of all those days when friends went well,
And see no half-friends lurking.

6

You know, you sometimes have
A sour look — I mean

You can be affable — but I have seen
Often on your face a look of —
Not exactly pain —

But more as if
Your dreams had lain
In puddles, stained
By themselves, like cigaret butts in the rain.

You look as if you came
From some other time
And idle in this calm
Remember storms you could not tame,
And feel at twenty years quite old
— But then, our tea is getting cold.

7

What storms have blown me, and from where,
What dreams have drowned, or half-dead, here
Surround me, or whether I am old or young,
I cannot find an answer on my tongue.
Yet if you ask me to describe that dark, wild
Winter of the eyes, then I
Can speak, answer endlessly,
For that look was not on me as a child.

Each year I lived I watched the fissure
Between what was and what I wished for
Widen, until there was nothing left
But the gulf of emptiness.
Most men have not seen the world divide,
Or seen, it did not open wide,
Or wide, they clung to the safer side.
But I have felt the sundering like a blade.

8

I am old
But quite perceptive —
I could have told
You many goals you strive
To reach
Are reachless, yet in some strange way
I feel there is nothing I can teach
Or do or say, but wheel my crippled age
Away, and let you wage
Your war.

9

I have been crouching here too long, sipping
Tea, while the souls I love, wan Troilus, old King
Lear fool-guided through the world, the noble
Prince, countless more, to tell
Too endless, Gib, Chris, and all, hold hell's
Hot breath back and summon me to battle.

Now I must nurse my courage in a sling,
I dream the ancient skies are ripening,
That golden fruit shall form like summer clouds
Demanding poet-men to sing like lords
Of giant gods who pace
The mountain-tops. Then I will write my peace.

Meditation among the Tombs

1

I am kneeling on my grave this lonely
Circle of the day or bottom half
Of night, to witness vainly
Day light candelabra on the dark horizons
Of the world. For this I tell my orisons
And char my tomb with incense for an epitaph.

The present darkness has been long,
And add, the clocks are closing down these days
Lacking a hand to push the hand ahead,
And you will hear the tick and thud
Begin to toil, as the roots of grass
Gnaw decomposition like a cud.

We who have won no issue from our dreams,
Who have never climbed the pale hills of dawn
Nor forged our fullness in the blaze of noon
Nor arched a crimson splendor down the west,
Scowl now at dark — curse God that our best
Is worse than what those grasses chew night-long.

2

Life like a coat of rose-colored paint
Is lifting from his lips. And in those eyes,
Glazed to seal their faint
Flames within, the last red coals

Sputter in his tears. "Try to raise
Your eyelids, gaze upon this cross, for souls
That burn such evil in their fires
Should quench themselves," two preachers bellow in his ears,
"With sorry vows instead of salty tears."

He flutters up those lids, but age
Has so bleared those weary
Eyes and the page
On which they register within
That the wrought and polished cross
Those phantoms wave before his chin
Seems but a pole to string its wires high
And shuttle back and forth love's perfidy.

Could such an antique hulk as this
Have ever opened eyes in wonderment of love
Or known the frenzy of a warded kiss?
It is very difficult to think.
And yet it seems he has enough
Old strings and yarns of memory to weave
A gaudy mess of dreams before he leaves.

Look, the glowing caves begin to blink:
What signals do they tell,
What dark suggestion in that skull
That life is twice, compared to death, as terrible?

3

Old Man: When youth was pounding in my veins
         And life was all a sky of light and dreams
         And none had any foresight for the pains
         A girl and I took love in summer's kiss
         Under the oak, half hidden in the grass.
Youth: There must have been much beauty in those flames.

Old Man: Later, when our love burned not so wild
          Or brilliant, but with a steady, subtle fuse
          And she was fevered with a coming child
          They said to me, "Choose you the living wife,
          Or risking her, the babe delivered safe?"
Youth: They might have chosen better word than choose.

Old Man: You who are young have no such memories
          Of trysting by that oak in the thick
          And shining grass, or kissing under skies
          Of singing wind. So which alternative,
          A dead creation or a dying love?
Youth: Creation is a sorry thing to pick.

4

Born,
My child, alas, so worn
And old, as though these eyes
Could stuff your sockets with their miseries . . .
I pray
That as your father and his father
Turned the waning cycle of their day,
Bending to the midnight mother
Heaped with age
And bitter with broken rage,
You will wind your days the other
And the better way: and as you near
The end, the furrows of your age will disappear
And everything that prods you to a sudden grave
Will take a counterclockwise turn,
Strange reversal you will learn,
Until your limbs are youthful, and your heart is brave.
And having said this prayer,
One word: to life's pretenders say you were
Descended from a line of vanished kings

Who sat in state upon a silver throne —
Then beat from that descent with careless wings
And of their depositions weave your crown.

5

The clock has spun while I have brooded here,
Spading up an earth of long-dead men —
Dry memory for a rainless year —
Is this a graveyard I am digging in?

But look, the dawn is lighting up the east,
The clouds are breaking, making way — soon!
Now! — through the dusk comes sliding fast,
Alas, that sullen orange eye, the moon.

The clock's two sentinels
Are dying, and midnight has begun again.
Lord, might we witness those castles
Surrender to the fair legions of the sun.

But if the darkness finds the graves where we
Were buried under sillions of our past
Still pointing gloomy crosses at the east,
And thinks that we were niggard with our bravery,
Our ghosts, if such we have, can say at least
We were not misers in our misery.

What a Kingdom It Was

To Charles and Diana Bell

PART I

First Song

Then it was dusk in Illinois, the small boy
After an afternoon of carting dung
Hung on the rail fence, a sapped thing
Weary to crying. Dark was growing tall
And he began to hear the pond frogs all
Calling on his ear with what seemed their joy.

Soon their sound was pleasant for a boy
Listening in the smoky dusk and the nightfall
Of Illinois, and from the fields two small
Boys came bearing cornstalk violins
And they rubbed the cornstalk bows with resins
And the three sat there scraping of their joy.

It was now fine music the frogs and the boys
Did in the towering Illinois twilight make
And into dark in spite of a shoulder's ache
A boy's hunched body loved out of a stalk
The first song of his happiness, and the song woke
His heart to the darkness and into the sadness of joy.

First Communion

The church is way over in the next county,
The same trip that last year we trekked
Carrying a sackful of ears to collect
The nickel-an-ear porcupine bounty.
Pictured on the wall over dark Jerusalem
Jesus is shining — in the dark he is a lamp.
On the tray he is a pastry wafer.
On the way home, there is regular talk˙
Of the fine preaching, before the regular jokes
Are allowed. The last time over
The same trail we brought two dollars homeward.
Now we carry the aftertaste of the Lord.
Soon a funny story about Uncle Abraham:
How, being liquored up, he got locked out
By his woman; how she must have taken blankets out
Later, for Sam says he found them, in the morning,
Asleep in each other's arms in the haybarn.

The sunlight streams through the afternoon
Another parable over the sloughs
And yellowing grass of the prairies.
Cold wind stirs, and the last green
Climbs to all the tips of the season, like
The last flame brightening on a wick.
Embers drop and break in sparks. Across the earth
Sleep is the overlapping of enough shadows.
In the wind outside a twig snaps
Like a tiny lid shutting somewhere in the ear.
Jesus, a boy thinks as his room goes out,
Jesus, it is a disappointing shed

Where they hang your picture
And drink juice, and conjure
Your person into inferior bread —
I would speak of injustice,
I would not go again into that place.

To Christ Our Lord

The legs of the elk punctured the snow's crust
And wolves floated lightfooted on the land
Hunting Christmas elk living and frozen;
Inside snow melted in a basin, and a woman basted
A bird spread over coals by its wings and head.

Snow had sealed the windows; candles lit
The Christmas meal. The Christmas grace chilled
The cooked bird, being long-winded and the room cold.
During the words a boy thought, is it fitting
To eat this creature killed on the wing?

He had killed it himself, climbing out
Alone on snowshoes in the Christmas dawn,
The fallen snow swirling and the snowfall gone,
Heard its throat scream as the gunshot scattered,
Watched it drop, and fished from the snow the dead.

He had not wanted to shoot. The sound
Of wings beating into the hushed air
Had stirred his love, and his fingers
Froze in his gloves, and he wondered,
Famishing, could he fire? Then he fired.

Now the grace praised his wicked act. At its end
The bird on the plate
Stared at his stricken appetite.
There had been nothing to do but surrender,
To kill and to eat; he ate as he had killed, with wonder.

At night on snowshoes on the drifting field
He wondered again, for whom had love stirred?
The stars glittered on the snow and nothing answered.
Then the Swan spread her wings, cross of the cold north,
The pattern and mirror of the acts of earth.

Burning

He lives, who last night flopped from a log
Into the creek, and all night lay pinned
To the water, drowned
But for the skin of the teeth of his dog.

I brought him boiled eggs and broth.
He coughed and waved his spoon
And sat up saying he would dine alone,
Being fatigue itself after that bath.

I sat outside in the sun with the dog.
Wearing a stocking on the ailing foot,
In monster crutches, he hobbled out,
And addressed the dog in bitter rage.

He told the yellow hound, his rescuer,
Its heart was bad, and it ought
Not wander by the creek at night;
If all his dogs got drowned he would be poor.

He stroked its head and disappeared in the shed
And came out with a stone mallet in his hands
And lifted that weight of many pounds
And let it fall on top of the dog's head.

I carted off the carcass, dug it deep.
Then he came too with what a thing to lug,
Or pour on a dog's grave, his thundermug,
And poured it out and went indoors to sleep.

I saw him sleepless in the pane of glass
Looking wild-eyed at sunset, then the glare
Blinded the glass — only a red square
Burning a house burning in the wilderness.

The Wolves

Last night knives flashed. LeChien cried
And chewed blood in his bed.
Vanni's whittling blade
Had found flesh easier than wood.

Vanni and I left camp on foot. In a glade
We came on a brown blossom
Great and shining on a thorned stem.
"That's the sensitive briar," I said.

"It shrinks at the touch," I added.
Soon we found buffalo. Picking
A bull grazing by itself, I began
The approach: while the shaggy head

Was turned I sprinted across the sod,
And when he swung around his gaze
I bellyflopped into the grass
And lay on my heartbeat and waited.

When he looked away again I made
Enough yardage before he wheeled
His head: I kneeled, levelled
My rifle, and we calmly waited.

It occurred to me as we waited
That in those last moments he was,
In fact, daydreaming about something else.
"He is too stupid to live," I said.

His legs shifted and the heart showed.
I fired. He looked, trotted off,
He simply looked and trotted off,
Stumbled, sat himself down, and became dead.

I looked for Vanni. Among the cows he stood,
Only his arms moving as he fired,
Loaded, and fired, the dumb herd
Milling about him sniffing at their dead.

I called and he retreated.
We cut two choice tongues for ourselves
And left the surplus. All day wolves
Would splash blood from those great sides.

Again we saw the flower, brown-red
On a thorn-spiked stem. When Vanni
Reached out his fingers, it was funny,
It shrank away as if it had just died.

They told us in camp that LeChien was dead.
None of us cared. Nobody much
Had liked him. His tobacco pouch,
I observed, was already missing from beside his bed.

Westport

From the hilltop we could overlook
The changes on the world. Behind us
Spread the forest, that half a continent away
Met our fathers on the Atlantic shore.
Before us lay a narrow belt of brush.
Everywhere beyond, shifting like an ocean,
Swell upon swell of emerald green,
The prairies of the west were blowing.

We mounted and set out, small craft
Into the green. The grasses brushed
The bellies of the horses, and under
The hooves the knotted centuries of sod
Slowed the way. Here and there the grey
Back of a wolf breached and fell, as in the grass
Their awkward voyages appeared and vanished.

Then rain lashed down in a savage squall.
All afternoon it drove us west. "It will be
A long, hard journey," the boy said, "and look,
We are blown like the weed." And indeed we were . . .
O wild indigo, O love-lies-bleeding,
You, prince's feather, pigweed, and bugseed,
Hold your ground as you can. We toss ahead
Of you in the wild rain, and we barely touch
The sad ambages compassed for yourselves.

When the storm abated, a red streak in the west
Lit up the raindrops on the land before us.
"Yes," I said, "it will be a hard journey . . ."

And the shining grasses were bowed towards the west
As if one craving had killed them. "But at last,"
I added, "the hardness is the thing you thank."
So out of forest we sailed onto plains,
And from the dark afternoon came a bright evening.

Now out of evening we discovered night
And heard the cries of the prairie and the moan
Of wind through the roots of its clinging flowers.

PART II

At the Reading of a Poet's Will

Item. A desk
Smelling of ink and turpentine
To anyone whose task
Is to sweat rain for a line.

Item. A sheaf
Of poems, a few lucid,
One or two brief,
To anyone who will bid.

*   *   *

Item. Praise Jesus, who spent
His last cent
In the wilderness of himself in the try
For self-mastery.

His boast
Is that though he did insist
On principle, in terror and compromise
He taught us what love's limit is.

Item. I built a desk,
I spent myself for a sheaf,
All else I committed I ask
That the Lord forgive.

I took Christ for my pattern,
Once he was kind to a slattern,
If I was led into mazes
Blame and praise Jesus. *Amen.*

Lilacs

The wind climbed with a laggard pace
Up the green hill, and meeting the sun there
Disappeared like warmed wax
Into the ground. Down on the south slope
A bitch stretched, and swaths of fierce lilacs
Opened huge furnaces of scent.

A woman betook herself into the park,
Her dry legs crackling in darkness
At bitch, lilac, the fierce and asleep.
Summer slopped at her knees,
The hot scent of herself beating herself
Out of closets in the well-governed flesh.

She stopped. The blossoms climbed
And blazed in the air, and the lawn slowly
Somersaulted under her. She turned back
To the narrow parlor, where tea and dry supper
Would be laid, and a spoon would arrange
The leaves on the bottom of her china dream.

A Toast to Tu Fu

To you, Tu Fu,
Because it didn't work out
When you lent
Yourself to government.
A poet isn't made to fix
Things up — only to celebrate
What's down, and in politics
As that Irishman found out
Is a lout.

To you, Tu Fu,
For fooling the crew
Who thought trial
Must make a man good;
And for, when the waters rose
Around the temple
You clung to in the flood,
While they prayed you'd
Let go with a prayer,
Having hung on like a bear.

And again to you, Tu Fu,
For gorging at the feast
Honoring your rescue,
For not mentioning virtue
In your short speech, nor praising rot,
And for having had the appetite and timing
To die of overeating on the spot.

Easter

We read of her death in the morning.
By the riverbank shreds of clothes and her purse.
Raped, robbed, weighted, drowned —
They conjecture the night-off of a virgin nurse.

To get to church you have to cross the river,
First breadwinner for the town, its wide
Mud-colored currents cleansing forever
The swill-making villages at its side.

The disinfected voice of the minister
For a moment is one of the clues,
But he is talking of nothing but Easter,
Dying so on the wood, He rose.

Some of us daydream of the morning news,
Some of us lament we rose at all,
A child beside me comforts her doll,
We are dying on the hard wood of the pews.

Death is everywhere, in the extensive
Sermon, the outcry of the inaudible
Prayer, the nickels, the dimes the poor give,
And outside, at last, in the gusts of April.

Upon the river, its Walden calm,
With wire hooks the little boats are fishing.
Those who can wait to get home
Line up, and lean on the railing, wishing.

Up through the mud can you see us
Waiting here for you, for hours,
Virgin lady, trapped or working loose,
Can you see our hats like a row of flowers?

Then we crown you with an Easter fire,
And if you do not rise before dinner
When the flower show must bow and retire,
Then drink well of the breadwinner,

And tomorrow when the brown water
Shall shove you senselessly on
Past smoking cities, works of disaster,
Kids playing ball, cows, unrealistic fishermen,

Toll bridges you slip under for free,
And you cast an eye from the brown lorry
Which floats your drenching flesh to sea,
Do not, moved by goodbyes, be altogether sorry

That the dream has ended. Turn
On the dream you lived through the unwavering gaze.
It is as you thought. The living burn.
In the floating days may you discover grace.

For William Carlos Williams

When you came and you talked and you read with your
Private zest from the varicose marble
Of the podium, the lovers of literature
Paid you the tribute of their almost total
Inattention, although someone when you spoke of a pig
Did squirm, and it is only fair to report another gig-

gled. But you didn't even care. You seemed
Above remarking we were not your friends.
You hung around inside the rimmed
Circles of your heavy glasses and smiled and
So passed a lonely evening. In an hour
Of talking your honesty built you a tower.

When it was over and you sat down and the chair-
man got up and smiled and congratulated
You and shook your hand, I watched a professor
In neat bow tie and enormous tweeds, who patted
A faint praise of the sufficiently damned,
Drained spittle from his pipe, then scrammed.

For the Lost Generation

Oddities composed the sum of the news.
$E = mc^2$
Was another weird
Sign of the existence of the Jews.

And Paris! All afternoon in someone's attic
We lifted our glasses
And drank to the asses
Who ran the world and turned neurotic.

Ours was a wonderful party,
Everyone threw rice,
The fattest girls were nice,
The world was rich in wisecracks and confetti.

The War was a first wife, somebody's blunder.
Who was right, who lost,
Held nobody's interest,
The dog on top was as bad as the dog under.

Sometimes after whiskey, at the break of day,
There was a trace
Of puzzlement on a face,
Face of blue nights that kept bleaching away.

Look back on it all — the faraway cost,
Crash and sweet blues
(O Hiroshima, O Jews) —
No generation was so gay as the lost.

Alewives Pool

1

We lay on the grass and heard
The world burning on the pulse of April,
And were so shaken and stirred, so cut, we wondered
Which things will we forget
And which remember always? We rose like birds

And flew down the path to the Alewives Pool
Where herring driven by lust from the seas
Came swarming until the pond would spill,
And fell amazed — how they memorize
Love's never-studied maps and ritual.

2

A dying woman from her bed once told
The row of faces dimming in her glance,
Who came to her party at four years old,
What frills each wore, who laughed, who could not dance,
Who cried, whose hand she would not let hers hold.

The infant searches at his mother's breast
Looking for the night he was shipwrecked from —
But when he finds her milk he suddenly tastes
A brightness that scares him, and his days to come
Flood on his heart as if they were his past.

3

Grass lies as though beating under the wind.
In the trees even the birds are astonished

By the passion of their song. The mind
Can only know what the blood has accomplished
When love has consumed it in the burning pond.

Now by the trembling water let death and birth
Flow through our selves as through the April grass —
The sudden summer this air flames forth
Makes us again into its blossomers —
Stand on the pulse and love the burning earth.

Leaping Falls

And so it was I sheered,
Eccentric, into outer space,
And tracked with lost paces
The forgotten journey of a child,
Across the creaking snow,
Up the deer-trail,

Over the snowdrifted hill
Into the secret country
Where a boy once found,
Routing from ledge to ledge
In a tumult at sunrise,
The downrush of Leaping Falls.

Now they were draped
Without motion or sound,
Icicles fastened in stories
To stillness and rock. Underneath,
A heap of icicles, broken,
Lay dead blue on the snow.

Cold was through and through,
Noiseless. Nothing
Except clouds at my nostrils
Moved. Then I uttered a word,
Simply a bleak word
Slid from the lips. Whereupon

A topmost icicle came loose
And fell, and struck another

With a bell-like sound, and
Another, and the falls
Leapt at their ledges, ringing
Down the rocks and on each other

Like an outbreak of bells
That rings and ceases.
The silence turned around
And became silence again.
Under the falls on the snow
A twigfire of icicles burned pale blue.

Promontory Moon

The moon: she shakes off her cloaks,
Her rings of mist and circle of blurred light,
And shines without chemistry or heat
Upon us. Milky blue in her influence
The sea rises dabbing at the tiers of rock.
A few shadowy rabbits move feinting
Over the grass and paths. In sunlight
Humans will sprawl generating on the grass;
But the rabbits ask nothing of the moon,
And run in moonlight for delight alone.

Half rabbits, half rabbits' shadows,
They are like the night-roistering fairies
For whom as children we set out banquets
In the dusk, of bits of bread and honey,
That we explored for in the dawn and found
Untouched, the one trace of fairies being
The dew glistening on the moss and grass
At daybreak, shed perhaps for sorrow
Their clearest bodies have no appetite,
Being woven by the night of moonlight.

The sun makes the grass increase, feeding
The things it can corrupt. The moon
Holds her purer watches on the night,
Mirroring on this fairest time of day
Only the miracles of light;
And that within ourselves too straight to bend
In agonies of death and birth — as now

66

The blue-white sea swirls at the moonbeams
And keeps on winding on the shining clew —
Dissolves at her touch and is weaved anew.

Across the Brown River

The Brown River, finger of a broken fist,
Moved sluggish through the woods and dust.
We made a bridge of the crashed oak, teetering
Across like monkeys taking up drinking,
Eschewing the deeps with our eyes,
For on the other side they said lay paradise.

It was a modern replica, built by the offspring of a rich
Dog-like dowager — some son-of-a-bitch
Who liked formal gardens of paths and shaven trees,
Hedges in a maze, and many elegant statues.
We noted "The Girl with Silk," a stone queen
With spread legs draped in the nick of time between.

In the afternoon we studied "The Last
Centaur Expiring," face folded on its breast,
All the segment that was a man pleading love
And fatal attraction for the brutal half.
A visitor beside us grew incensed
At miscegenation, and spoke out bitterly against.

We went our way at last, dancing across the oak
Into the woods. From the woods outside of Eden came a snake.
We found no principle of evil here except
Tweed packed with butter halted where it stepped,
Binoculars fixed on birds fleeing in the trees
The narrow eye bloated in the goggles of paradise.

Gothic Slide

Above the blue wash of the lake
Where the sun is a bright spectre,
And cars run, we discourse on culture;
Now the curtains close our modern talk
And faces in the slides revive
World-famous beauty, blent of light and grief.
Who can look on the stone figures,
The fatal innocence in the stone smiles,
And not sit by the feet of desire, a credulous pupil?
Over the cloaked body and covered neck
The lips come alive, but they move alone;
How can we speak with tongues made of stone?
The curtains open and our dazed eyes wreck
On the sheer sunlight climbing like a dream
Into the darkness which had become our home.
Below, the waves return like breath
To the shores of Chicago; sunlight weaves
In flashes over the curve of the Drive
Where the cars and cares of the earth
Crawl in a line. Is it this to be human —
A flair for the ideal gone bad under the breastbone?

One Generation

A girl of twenty walks with a gray-
haired man, her lover, a book of narrow verse
In his hand. In the sunset they sink
Down the slope together, tied
Into a knot of love, to be undone
Only by extremes and crying, and then
Never done again. An old man reads a newspaper
On the hill; not far off a little girl. The night
Comes over them. And I
Alone on the grass: what if I now should
Touch your face, child, mother, star first and faint in the sky?

Earth-Sparrow

The trees in clouds of November mist
Standing empty and the massive earth bare
I bent my head and leaned myself against
Interior gales and blizzards of unrest
Facing the squalor of November air

But stopped at last and skyward with shredded
Arms lifting ribbons of fingers and prayers
I caught in that beseeching of the cloud
One leafless lightning-splintered oak unshroud-
ing its wreckage in the waste of the year

To whose ultimate twig with a glide and
Skip a sparrow summitted and there burst-
ing as if the dead sap kept singing leaned
I forward knowing nothing to lean on
Green as the grasslessness Lord of the earth.

Rain over a Continent

Rain over a continent, the train
From Washington to Washington plunged
In the sowing rain. He slept with
His nurse on the voyage, she was rough,
Scarred with transcontinental love,
She was his all-guessing heart when he died.
Raise the blind, he commanded. Under
The rain the continent wheeled, his own land
Electric and blind, farmlights and cities'
Blazes — points, clusters and chains —
Each light a memory and the whole of darkness
Memory. In the seedfall of a continent
The majesty of a man rendered himself home:
His death was dust on the land when he died.

Reply to the Provinces

He writes from the provinces: it is
Shuttered and desolate there, will I please
Sit on a bench for him every so often
In the Luxembourg Gardens? So now
In the elegant autumn, to regard and guess —

The sea-eyed children watching their sloops
Angling on the pond? Expectant in their books
The delicate young women? The would-be
Casters-off of expectation? The hands-in-hands?
The fellow shucking chestnuts for his girl?
The Algerians, Americans, English, Danes
Giving the Gardens their Parisian character?
Fountained light streaming on the wind?
Surely these and things of this kind —
Whatever is human. Also I marvel at the leaves
Yellow on the sky, and there on the grass
Where the leaves overlap, yellow, the yellow sun
Forcing a hidden glowing from the earth —
I peer like an ape on a branch, on a bench —

In the provinces he may have walked from town.
In a city of leaves he may have found her. Perhaps
Already they are lying in the leaves, laughing,
Pointing out for each other the brown faces in the leaves.

Near Barbizon

At first I thought some animal, wounded,
Thrashed in the brush, for the hunting horns
Had sounded last night and this morning.
No, it was only the little woodgatherer
Out after lunch for twigs for the fire.
He had his own way of breaking a branch.
Others might have laid it across two rocks
And jumped in the middle. He raised it like a flail
And beat a rock until the weapon broke.
We talked. It was election time, and I asked
Whom was he voting for. He screwed his eyes.
"If there came into your house by night
Thieves, to which would you offer your wife?"
Whacks he laid on the rock until the branch gave.
"I am too honest, *merde*, or too poor to vote.
There's fuel on the forest floor still."
"What's your trade?" I inquired. "Gardener."
"So you make things bloom?" "Yes, and the pay's
Nothing." He was flailing the rocks in savage, measured
Strokes. "The pay's nothing," he repeated,
Looking up without ceasing his labor, keys of both
Eyes flashing, this intellectual, this rich American, this fascist boss!

Duck-Chasing

I spied a very small brown duck
Riding the swells. "Little duck!"
I cried. It paddled away,
I paddled after it. When it dived,
Down I dived too: too smoky was the sea,
We were lost. It surfaced
In the west, I swam west
And when it dived I dived,
And we were lost and lost and lost
In the slant smoke of the sea.
When I came floating up on it
From the side, like a deadman,
And yelled suddenly, it took off,
It skimmed the swells as it ascended,
Brown wings burning and flashing
In the sun as the sea it rose over
Burned and flashed underneath it.
I did not see the little duck again.
Duck-chasing is a game like any game.
When it is over it is all over.

For Ruth

It was a surprise,
Seeing you. You were
More steadfast than I remember.
On the limestone shelf
You endured yourself
With grace.

The shock was only
When you laid in on tape
Some of my speech, to escape
Into or to live through
Later on, when you would get blue —
But of course you would be lonely,

You of that fierce memory!
I saw you once remembering
A fisherman drunk as bait on a string
At the end of the bar —
Your chilled flesh went blue as a star.
A thing turns real for you eventually,

The touch is just the babytooth.
On your heap of bleached rock
You listen, wires in the mind play it back,
You hear the million sighs,
You cry for them, each simply cries
For ruth, for ruth.

In a Parlor Containing a Table

In a parlor containing a table
And three chairs, three men confided
Their inmost thoughts to one another.
I, said the first, am miserable.
I am miserable, the second said.
I think that for me the correct word
Is miserable, asserted the third.
Well, they said at last, it's quarter to two.
Good night. Cheer up. Sleep well.
You too. You too. You too.

Guillaume de Lorris

His is the romance without a heroine —
Only the Rose in the Garden, far away,
Restless in shadows, longing to be plucked.
The intensity of his dream nourishing him
The hero walks the desert of this world
Towards, without swerving, *l'idéale Bien-Aimée.*

He comes into the Garden on broken feet
After many years: he discovers at last,
Unattended, the single, mysterious Rose.
Being old at this moment (he has walked
Half his life on the desert), he declines,
Out of pity, to take what he has just to take.

Suddenly, however, he remembers the quest —
The days of solitude, when everywhere,
It seemed, others were happy on the earth.
Old in his heart, grown pale as the desert,
He looks for the Rose. He sees her in the arms
Of young men, and she is shedding tears for him.

Towards the Wilderness

Trekking the desert the man feels
The atmosphere on him like a knapsack.
He knows the fix upon him of eyes
Hung from huge wings frayed at the edges
Floating dead and black in the sky.

And the Dead Sea, that will neither
Renew nor drown him, a glow rubbed
Into the sand, shimmers under the range
In which Nebo can be picked out
As the historic, tall, and bleak one.

He puts the bead of his will on the peak
And does not waver. He is dying:
His plan is to look over the far side
Of the hill on which Moses died looking this way,
And to see the bitter land, and to die of desire.

PART III

The Schoolhouse

1

I find it now, the schoolhouse by the tree,
And through the broken door, in brown light,
I see the benches in rows, the floor he
Paced across, the windows where the fruit
Took the shapes of hearts, and the leaves windled
In the fall, and winter snowed on his head.

In this wreck of a house we were taught
Everything we imagined a man could know,
All action, all passion, all ancient thought,
What Socrates had got from Diotima,
How Troilus laughed, in tears, in paradise,
That crowns leapfrog through blood: casts of the dice.

The door hangs from one hinge. Maybe the last
Schoolboy simply forgot to lift the latch
When he rushed out that spring, in his haste —
Or maybe the same one, now fat and rich,
Snow-haired in his turn, and plagued by thought,
Broke his way back in, looking for the dead light.

2

A man of letters once asked the local tramps
To tea. No one came, and he read from Otway
And Chatterton to the walls, and lived for months
On tea. They padlocked the gate when he died.

Snow, sleet, rain, the piss of tramps; and one year
The lock snapped, the gate rasped open like a rooster.

And now when the tramps wake sheeted in frost,
They know it is time, they come here and sprawl
At the foot of the statue of their host
Which they call "His Better Self," which he had called
"Knowledge," sometimes "Death," whose one gesture
Seems to beckon and yet remains obscure,

And boil their tea on the floor and pick fruit
In the garden where that man used to walk
Thinking of Eden and the fallen state,
And dust an apple as he had a book —
"Hey now Porky, gie's the core," one hollers;
"Wise up," says Pork, "they ain't gonna *be* a core."

3

I hear modern schoolchildren shine their pants
In buttock-blessing seats in steamy schools
Soaking up civics and vacant events
From innocents who sponge periodicals
And squeeze that out again in chalky gray
Across the blackboards of the modern day;

Yet they can guess why we fled our benches
Afternoons when we ourselves were just nice
Schoolkids too, who peered out through the branches
For one homely share of the centuries
— Fighting in Latin the wars of the Greeks —
Our green days, the apple we picked and picked

And that was never ours; though they would
Rake their skulls if they found out we returned
By free choice to this house of the dead,
And stand here wondering what he could have learned,

His eyes great pupils and his fishhook teeth
Sunk in the apple of knowledge or death.

4

I recall a recitation in that house:
"We are the school of Hellas was the claim.
Maybe it was so. Anyway Hellas
Thought it wasn't, and put the school to flame.
They came back, though, and sifted the ruin."
I think the first inkling of the lesson

Was when we watched him from the apple wrest
Something that put the notion in his brain
The earth was coming to its beautifulest
And would be just like paradise again
The day he died from it. The flames went out
In the blue mantles; he waved us to the night —

And we are here, under the starlight. I
Remember he taught us the stars disperse
In wild flight, though constellated to the eye.
And now I can see the night in its course,
The slow sky uncoiling in exploding forms,
The stars that flee it riding free in its arms.

Seven Streams of Nevis

I

Jack the Blindman, whose violin
Down the harsh weathers of the street
Lifted a scraping bright and sweet,
Joked the sad bars of every tune;
Hardly a dime ever drops there
And he cups *faith* in the clankless air.

Connelly, one-eyed, half blind,
Finding the world blind, in full view
Like wind blew ropes and fences through.
Ticketless at the stiles of the mind
We ask his *hope:* down, and out,
To swear, "If scum swims to the top of the sauerkraut . . ."

They didn't sign up at the desk
Or queue at the bed, though they clapped
The night you bumped and shook and slapped
And ground for free your smart burlesque,
Peaches. We call it *mercy* when
You give and get nothing and give again.

Tossing in dreams young David Boyle
Could not evade the call of the Lord
For the meek life. He woke and poured
Over his heart the scalding oil
Of *temperance.* Now in his sleep
He yells aloud to God to let him sleep.

Justice made James Lynch Fitzstephen
Hang from a tree his guilty son;
His heart, twice guilty then,
Hanged itself in his skeleton.
Even Cicero would have known
The unjust who are just are just mad bone.

Natasha, who billowed like silk
On a pole of fire, and weeping went
To one who scrapes the burning tent
While he puffs Luckies and sips milk,
And came home like an empty cage
To find home yet emptier, tried *courage.*

Sir Henry, seeing that the dew
Gets burned each morning into mist,
Decided fire brings out the best
In things, and that anyone who
Has cooked his eyes at the sunrise
Of the beautiful, and thumbed himself blind, is *wise.*

2

In darkness I climbed Ben Nevis, far from
Your lives. But the seven streams I came on
Were well foreknown. One sang like strings, one crashed
Through gated rocks, one vibrated, others
Went skipping like unbucketed grease across
Hot stones, or clattered like bones, or like milk
Spilled and billowed in streamers of bright silk,
Irises glimmering a visionary course —
Me grimping the dark, sniffing for the source;
And there I found it windless, lying still,
Dark, high-nested in the mountain, a pool
Whose shined waters on the blackened mountain
Mirrored the black skies; and I rode out on the water
And the waves ringing through the dark were the rings

Around the eye itself of the world, which,
Drawing down heaven like its black lid, was there
Where merely to be still was temperate,
Where to move was brave, where justice was a glide,
Knowledge the dissolving of the head-hung eyes;
And there my faith lay burning, there my hope
Lay burning on the water, there charity
Burned like a sun. Oh give, O pool of heaven,
The locus of grace to seven who are whirled
Down the eddies and gutters of the world;
And Connelly and Jack and Peaches, Dave,
Lynch, Natalie, and Hank — seven who have
Bit on your hearts, and spat the gravels of
Tooth and heart, and bit again; who have wiped
The thumb-burst jellies of eyes on a sleeve
(The visions we could have wrung from that cloth)
And sprouted sight like mushrooms — O seven
Streams of nothing backgazing after heaven,
In the heart's hell you have it; call it God's Love.

The Descent

I

Nailed by our axes to the snow
We belayed. One by one we climbed.
Had somebody in the valley
Been looking up, it must have seemed
Some crazy earthworm headed for paradise,
Or else, if he happened to rub his eyes

While we unroped, and to look back
When we had scattered in the race
For the crest, an ascension of crows.
I took the crest as the day broke,
Sure I was first. But Jan must have leapt
The crevasse for a shortcut: he lay there,

Blue lips apart, on the blue snow,
Sprawled on the shellbursts of his heart.
"It's time it went," he gasped. Four years
He had fought in the guerilla wars.
Then he whispered, "Look — the sunrise!"
The same color and nearly the same size,

But behind his back, the sun
Was rising. When the moon he was
Staring at set in the mountains
He died. On the way down the ice
Had turned so perilous under the sun
There was no choice: we watched while he went down.

2

In Seekonk Woods, on Indian Hill,
It used to seem the branches made
A small green sky that gave off shade.
Once while I lay buried like a quail
In the grass and shadows, a shotgun
Banged, leaves burst, I blinked into the sunshine —

Two crows blown out from either hand
Went clattering away; a third
Thumped through the branches to the ground.
I scooped it up, splashed across the ford,
And lit out — I must have run half a day
Before I reached Holy Spring. (Anyway,

I thought it was holy. No one
Had told me heaven is overhead.
I only knew people look down
When they pray.) I held the dying bird
As though, should its heartbeat falter,
There wouldn't be any heartbeat anywhere.

After a while I touched the plumes
To the water. In the desert
By the tracks I dug a headstart
Taller than myself. I told him,
"Have a good journey, crow. It can't be far.
It'll be way this side of China, for sure."

3

And had I faced Jan to the sun
Might not the sun have held him here?
Or did he know the day came on
Behind, not glancing back for fear
The moon already was dragging from his bones
The blood as dear to them, and as alien,

As the suit of clothes to a scarecrow
Or the flesh to a cross? Down snow,
Following streambeds through the trees,
We sledded him. To his valleys
Rivers have washed this climber to the sun
The full moon pestled into earth again.

Heaven is in light, overhead,
I have it by heart. Yet the dead
Silting the darkness do not ask
For burials elsewhere than the dusk.
They lie where nothing but the moon can rise,
And make no claims, though they had promises.

Milkweed that grow beside the tombs
Climb from the dead as if in flight,
But a foot high they stop and bloom
In drab shapes, that neither give light
Nor bring up the true darkness of the dead;
Strange, homing lamps, that go out seed by seed.

4

I looked for Indian Hill at Easter.
It was bulldozed. A TV cross
Gleamed from the rooftop of a house
Like sticks of a scarecrow. Once more
I turned and ran: I stumbled on
Fields lying dark and savage and the sun

Reaping its own fire from the trees,
Whirling the faint panic of birds
Up turbulent light. Two white-haired
Crows cried under the wheeling rays;
And loosed as by a scythe, into the sky
A flight of jackdaws rose, earth-birds suddenly

Seized by some thaumaturgic thirst,
Shrill wings flung up the crow-clawed, burned,
Unappeasable air. And one turned,
Dodged through the flock again and burst
Eastward alone, sinking across the trees
On the world-curve of its wings. So it is,

Mirrored in duskfloods, the fisherbird
Stands in a desolate sky
Feeding at its own heart. In the cry
Eloi! Eloi! flesh was made word:
We hear it in wind catching in the branches.
In lost blood breaking a night through the bones.

Where the Track Vanishes

1

The snow revives in the apple trees;
The winter sun seeps from jonquils
Bright as goldmills on the slopes;
Le chemin montant dans les hautes herbes
Curves for the Alps and vanishes.

2

Pierre le Boiteux
— Yellow teeth
Gnashed into gum-level
Stumps, yellow
Eyes beaconing about,
A blackhead the size
Of a huckleberry
Making a cheek sag,
A leg gypsies
Cut the tendon of
So he could beg as a child
Pumping under him,
Twelve goats at heel —
Mounts the track,
Limping through the wild
Grasses — toward where?

3

The track vanishes in a heap of stones
Mortared by weeds and wildflowers —

The fallen church. Nearby stand stones
Of the parish graves, dates worn away,
A handful of carved words visible:
Jacques et Geneviève, priez pour eux —
Véronique DuPrès, regrets éternels —
Sown here even to their fingertips.

Who was it wore the track through the grass?
Surely their mourners are dead, and theirs, and theirs.
Perhaps Pierre limps up every day
Training the goats where to come when it is time,
Foreseeing the terrible loneliness.
No one is lonely here: take Véronique — Jacques,
Husband of another, indifferently dissolves into her.
A skull or two, a couple of pelvises or knees.

4

My hand on the sky
Cannot shut the sky out
Any more than any March
Branch can. In the Boston Store
Once, I tried new shoes:
The shoeman put my feet
Into a machine, saying Kid
Wrig yer toes. I
Wrigged and peered:
Inside green shoes green
Twigs were wrigging by themselves
Green as the grasses
I drew from her
Hair in the springtime
While she laughed, unfoliaged
By sunlight, a little
Spray of bones I loved.

5

From villages lost in the valleys —
Moncharvet, St. Bon, La Jaura —
Thin braids of smoke waver upward
Through the clear air. A few lights
Come on, visible from the untracked snow
On the stairway to the Alps. Venus
Shines from the grave of the sun, like
The white gem churched again in its valley.

Once driving from Morristown at night,
We came over a crest: the Fish-Island
Breached shining under the strung-out stars
Of the Galaxy — a long way from Jacques
And Geneviève and Véronique in her prairie.
We stood there not thinking that for them
This was a strange continent to be dying in,
This island under the continent of the stars —

Job's Coffin and the Scorpion; Jacques
And Geneviève side by side in the field of light;
Capricorn, Ophiocus; the Serpent embracing
The unhinged knees, St. Bon heaped
In its molted skin; Le Fourmier the arms
Of Hercules; the Swan sailing toward Planay;
Moncharvet, La Jaura by the singing Lyre,
Véronique rocked on the Balances; Champ Béranger —

Fields into which the Herdsman limps
Leading his flock up the trackless night, towards
A writhing of lights. Are they Notre Dame des Neiges
Where men ask their God for the daily bread —
Or the March-climbing Virgin carrying wheat?
Where the track vanishes the first land begins.
It goes out everywhere obliterating the horizons.
We must have been walking through it all our lives.

Freedom, New Hampshire

I

We came to visit the cow
Dying of fever,
Towle said it was already
Shovelled under, in a secret
Burial-place in the woods.
We prowled through the woods
Weeks, we never

Found where. Other
Children other summers
Must have found the place
And asked, Why is it
Green here? The rich
Guess a grave, maybe,
The poor think a pit

For dung, like the one
We shovelled in in the fall
That came up green
The next year, that may as well
Have been the grave
Of a cow or something
For all that shows. A child guesses
By whether his house has a bathroom.

2

We found a cowskull once; we thought it was
From one of the asses in the Bible, for the sun

Shone into the holes through which it had seen
Earth as an endless belt carrying gravel, had heard
Its truculence cursed, had learned how sweat
Stinks, and had brayed — shone into the holes
With solemn and majestic light, as if some
Skull somewhere could be Baalbek or the Parthenon.

That night passing Towle's Barn
We saw lights. Towle had lassoed a calf
By its hind legs, and he tugged against the grip
Of the darkness. The cow stood by chewing millet.
Derry and I took hold, too, and hauled.
It was sopping with darkness when it came free.
It was a bullcalf. The cow mopped it awhile,
And we walked around it with a lantern,

And it was sunburned, somehow, and beautiful.
It took a dug as the first business
And sneezed and drank at the milk of light.
When we got it balanced on its legs, it went wobbling
Towards the night. Walking home in darkness
We saw the July moon looking on Freedom New Hampshire,
We smelled the fall in the air, it was the summer,
We thought, Oh this is but the summer!

3
Once I saw the moon
Drift into the sky like a bright
Pregnancy pared
From a goddess who thought
To be beautiful she must keep slender —
Cut loose, and drifting up there
To happen by itself —
And waning, in lost labor;

As we lost our labor
Too — afternoons

When we sat on the gate
By the pasture, under the Ledge,
Buzzing and skirling on toilet-
papered combs tunes
To the rumble-seated cars
Taking the Ossipee Road

On Sundays; for
Though dusk would come upon us
Where we sat, and though we had
Skirled out our hearts in the music,
Yet the dandruffed
Harps we skirled it on
Had done not much better than
Flies, which buzzed, when quick

We trapped them in our hands,
Which went silent when we
Crushed them, which we bore
Downhill to the meadowlark's
Nest full of throats
Which Derry charmed and combed
With an Arabian air, while I
Chucked crushed flies into

Innards I could not see,
For the night had fallen
And the crickets shrilled on all sides
In waves, as if the grassleaves
Shrieked by hillsides
As they grew, and the stars
Made small flashes in the sky,
Like mica flashing in rocks

On the chokecherried Ledge
Where bees I stepped on once
Hit us from behind like a shotgun,
And where we could see

Windowpanes in Freedom flash
And Loon Lake and Winnipesaukee
Flash in the sun
And the blue world flashing.

4

The fingerprints of our eyeballs would zigzag
On the sky; the clouds that came drifting up
Our fingernails would drift into the thin air;
In bed at night there was music if you listened,
Of an old surf breaking far away in the blood.

Children who come by chance on grass green for a man
Can guess cow, dung, man, anything they want,
To them it is the same. To us who knew him as he was
After the beginning and before the end, it is green
For a name called out of the confusions of the earth —

Winnipesaukee coined like a moon, a bullcalf
Dragged from the darkness where it breaks up again,
Larks which long since have crashed for good in the grass
To which we fed the flies, buzzing ourselves like flies,
While the crickets shrilled beyond us, in July . . .

The mind may sort it out and give it names —
When a man dies he dies trying to say without slurring
The abruptly decaying sounds. It is true
That only flesh dies, and spirit flowers without stop
For men, cows, dung, for all dead things; and it is good, yes —

But an incarnation is in particular flesh
And the dust that is swirled into a shape
And crumbles and is swirled again had but one shape
That was this man. When he is dead the grass
Heals what he suffered, but he remains dead,
And the few who loved him know this until they die.

For my brother, 1925–1957

99

The Supper after the Last

1

The desert moves out on half the horizon
Rimming the illusory water which, among islands,
Bears up the sky. The sea scumbles in
From its own inviolate border under the sky.
A dragon-fly floating on six legs on the sand
Lifts its green-yellow tail, declines its wings
A little, flutters them a little, and lays
On dazzled sand the shadow of its wings. Near shore
A bather wades through his shadow in the water.
He tramples and kicks it; it recomposes.

2

Outside the open door
Of the whitewashed house,
Framed in its doorway, a chair,
Vacant, waits in the sunshine.

A jug of fresh water stands
Inside the door. In the sunshine
The chair waits, less and less vacant.
The host's plan is to offer water, then stand aside.

3

They eat *rosé* and chicken. The chicken head
Has been tucked under the shelter of the wing.
Under the table a red-backed, passionate dog
Cracks chicken bones on the blood and gravel floor.

No one else but the dog and the blind
Cat watching it knows who is that bearded
Wild man guzzling overhead, the wreck of passion
Emptying his eyes, who has not yet smiled,

Who stares at the company, where he is company,
Turns them to sacks of appalled, grinning skin,
Forks the fowl-eye out from under
The large, makeshift, cooked lid, evaporates the wine,

Jellies the sunlit table and spoons, floats
The deluxe grub down the intestines of the Styx,
Devours all but the cat and the dog, to whom he slips scraps,
The red-backed accomplice busy grinding gristle.

4

When the bones of the host
Crack in the hound's jaw
The wild man rises. Opening
His palms he announces:
I came not to astonish
But to destroy you. Your
Jug of cool water? Your
Hanker after wings? Your
Lech for transcendence?
I came to prove you are
Intricate and simple things
As you are, created
In the image of nothing,
Taught of the creator
By your images in dirt —
As mine, for which you set
A chair in the sunshine,
Mocking me with water!
As pictures of wings,
Not even iridescent,

That clasp the sand
And that cannot perish, you swear,
Having once been evoked!

5

The witnesses back off; the scene begins to float in water;
Far out in that mirage the Saviour sits whispering to the world,
Becoming a mirage. The dog turns into a smear on the sand.
The cat grows taller and taller as it flees into space.

From the hot shine where he sits his whispering drifts:
You struggle from flesh into wings; the change exists.
But the wings that live gripping the contours of the dirt
Are all at once nothing, flesh and light lifted away.

You are the flesh; I am the resurrection, because I am the light.
I cut to your measure the creeping piece of darkness
That haunts you in the dirt. Step into light —
I make you over. I breed the shape of your grave in the dirt.

PART IV

The Avenue Bearing the Initial of Christ into the New World

Was diese kleine Gasse doch für ein Reich an sich war . . .

I

pcheek pcheek pcheek pcheek pcheek
They cry. The motherbirds thieve the air
To appease them. A tug on the East River
Blasts the bass-note of its passage, lifted
From the infra-bass of the sea. A broom
Swishes over the sidewalk like feet through leaves.
Valerio's pushcart Ice Coal Kerosene
Moves   clack
         clack
           clack
On a broken wheelrim. Ringing in its chains
The New Star Laundry horse comes down the street
Like a roofleak whucking into a pail.
At the redlight, where a horn blares,
The Golden Harvest Bakery brakes on its gears,
Squeaks, and seethes in place. A propane-
gassed bus makes its way with big, airy sighs.

Across the street a woman throws open
Her window,
She sets, terribly softly,
Two potted plants on the windowledge
      tic   tic
And bangs shut her window.

A man leaves a doorway tic toc tic toc tic toc tic hurrah
    toc splat on Avenue C tic etc and turns the corner.

Banking the same corner
A pigeon coasts 5th Street in shadows,
Looks for altitude, surmounts the rims of buildings,
And turns white.

The babybirds pipe down. It is day.

2

In sunlight on the Avenue
The Jew rocks along in a black fur shtraimel,
Black robe, black knickers, black knee-stockings,
Black shoes. His beard like a sod-bottom
Hides the place where he wears no tie.
A dozen children troop after him, barbels flying,
In skullcaps. They are Reuben, Simeon, Levi, Judah, Issachar,
        Zebulun, Benjamin, Dan, Naphtali, Gad, Asher.
With the help of the Lord they will one day become
Courtiers, thugs, rulers, rabbis, asses, adders, wrestlers,
        bakers, poets, cartpushers, infantrymen.

The old man is sad-faced. He is near burial
And one son is missing. The women who bore him sons
And are past bearing, mourn for the son
And for the father, wondering if the man will go down
Into the grave of a son mourning, or if at the last
The son will put his hands on the eyes of his father.

The old man wades towards his last hour.
On 5th Street, between Avenues A and B,
In sunshine, in his private cloud, Bunko Certified Embalmer,
Cigar in his mouth, nose to the wind, leans
At the doorway of Bunko's Funeral Home & Parlour,
Glancing west towards the Ukrainians, eastward idly
Where the Jew rocks towards his last hour.

Sons, grandsons at his heel, the old man
Confronts the sun. He does not feel its rays

Through his beard, he does not understand
Fruits and vegetables live by the sun.
Like his children he is sallow-faced, he sees
A blinding signal in the sky, he smiles.

Bury me not Bunko damned Catholic I pray you in Egypt.

3

From the Station House
Under demolishment on Houston
To the Power Station on 14th,
Jews, Negroes, Puerto Ricans
Walk in the spring sunlight.

The Downtown Talmud Torah
Blosztein's Cutrate Bakery
Areceba Panataria Hispano
Peanuts Dried Fruit Nuts & Canned Goods
Productos Tropicales
Appetizing Herring Candies Nuts
Nathan Kugler Chicken Store Fresh Killed Daily
Little Rose Restaurant
Rubinstein the Hatter Mens Boys Hats Caps Furnishings
J. Herrmann Dealer in All Kinds of Bottles
Natural Bloom Cigars
Blony Bubblegum
Mueren las Cucarachas Super Potente Garantizada de Matar las
          Cucarachas mas Resistentes
Wenig מצבות
G. Schnee Stairbuilder
Everyouth la Original Loción Eterna Juventud Satisfacción Dinero
          Devuelto
Happy Days Bar & Grill

Through dust-stained windows over storefronts
Curtains drawn aside, onto the Avenue

Thronged with Puerto Ricans, Negroes, Jews,
Baby carriages stuffed with groceries and babies,
The old women peer, blessed damozels
Sitting up there young forever in the cockroached rooms,
Eating fresh-killed chicken, productos tropicales,
Appetizing herring, canned goods, nuts;
They puff out smoke from Natural Bloom cigars
And one day they puff like Blony Bubblegum.

From a rooftop a boy fishes at the sky,
Around him a flock of pigeons fountains,
Blown down and swirling up again, seeking the sky.
A red kite wriggles like a tadpole
Into the sky beyond them, crosses
The sun, lays bare its own crossed skeleton.

To fly from this place — to roll
On some bubbly blacktop in the summer,
To run under the rain of pigeon plumes, to be
Tarred, and feathered with birdshit, Icarus,

In Kugler's glass headdown dangling by yellow legs.

4

First Sun Day of the year. Tonight,
When the sun will have turned from the earth,
She will appear outside Hy's Luncheonette,
The crone who sells the *News* and the *Mirror,*
The oldest living thing on Avenue C,
Outdating much of its brick and mortar.
If you ask for the *News* she gives you the *Mirror*
And squints long at the nickel in her hand
Despising it, perhaps, for being a nickel,
And stuffs it in her apron pocket
And sucks her lips. Rain or stars, every night
She is there, squatting on the orange crate,
Issuing out only in darkness, like the cucarachas

And strange nightmares in the chambers overhead.
She can't tell one newspaper from another,
She has forgotten how Nain her dead husband looked,
She has forgotten her children's whereabouts
Or how many there were, or what the *News*
And *Mirror* tell about that we buy them with nickels.
She is sure only of the look of a nickel
And that there is a Lord in the sky overhead.
She dwells in a flesh that is of the Lord
And drifts out, therefore, only in darkness
Like the streetlamp outside the Luncheonette
Or the lights in the secret chamber
In the firmament, where Yahweh himself dwells.
Like Magdalene in the Battistero of Saint John
On the carved-up continent, in the land of sun,
She lives shadowed, under a feeble bulb
That lights her face, her crab's hands, her small bulk on the crate.

She is Pulchería mother of murderers and madmen,
She is also Alyona whose neck was a chicken leg.

Mother was it the insufferable wind?
She sucks her lips a little further into the mousehole.
She stares among the stars, and among the streetlamps.

The mystery is hers.

5

That violent song of the twilight!
Now, in the silence, will the motherbirds
Be dead, and the infantbirds
That were in the dawn merely transparent
Unfinished things, nothing but bellies,
Will they have been shoved out
And in the course of a morning, casually,
On scrawny wings, have taken up the life?

6

In the pushcart market, on Sunday,
A crate of lemons discharges light like a battery.
Icicle-shaped carrots that through black soil
Wove away lie like flames in the sun.
Onions with their shirts ripped seek sunlight
On green skins. The sun beats
On beets dirty as boulders in cowfields,
On turnips pinched and gibbous
From budging rocks, on embery sweets,
On Idahos, Long Islands and Maines,
On horseradishes still growing weeds on the flat ends,
On cabbages lying about like sea-green brains
The skulls have been shucked from,
On tomatoes, undented plum-tomatoes, alligator-skinned
Cucumbers, that float pickled
In the wooden tubs of green skim milk —

Sky-flowers, dirt-flowers, underdirt-flowers,
Those that climbed for the sun in their lives
And those that wormed away — equally uprooted,
Maimed, lopped, shucked, and misaimed.

In the market in Damascus a goat
Came to a stall where twelve goatheads
Were lined up for sale. It sniffed them
One by one. Finally thirteen goats started
Smiling in their faintly sardonic way.

A crone buys a pickle from a crone,
It is wrapped in the *Mirror,*
At home she will open the wrapping, stained,
And stare and stare and stare at it.

And the cucumbers, and the melons,
And the leeks, and the onions, and the garlic.

7

Already the Avenue troughs the light of day.
Southwards, towards Houston and Pitt,
Where Avenue C begins, the eastern ranges
Of the wiped-out lives — punks, lushes,
Panhandlers, pushers, rumsoaks, everyone
Who took it easy when he should have been out failing at some
        thing —
The pots-and-pans man pushes his cart,
Through the intersection of the light, at 3rd,
Where sunset smashes on the aluminum of it,
On the bottoms, curves, handles, metal panes,
Mirrors: of the bead-curtained cave under the falls
In Freedom, Seekonk Woods leafing the light out,
Halfway to Kingston where a road branched out suddenly,
Between Pamplonne and Les Salins two meeting paths
Over a sea the green of churchsteeple copper.
Of all places on earth inhabited by men
Why is it we find ourselves on this Avenue
Where the dusk gets worse,
And the mirrorman pushing his heaped mirrors
Into the shadows between 3rd and 2nd,
Pushes away a mess of old pots and pans?

The ancient Negro sits as usual
Outside the Happy Days Bar & Grill. He wears
Dark glasses. Every once in a while, abruptly,
He starts to sing, chanting in a hoarse, nearly breaking
Voice —

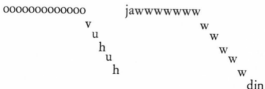

And becomes silent
    Stares into the polaroid Wilderness

III

Gross-Rosen, Maidanek, Flössenberg, Ravensbruck, Stutthof, Riga,
Bergen-Belsen, Mauthausen, Birkenau, Treblinka, Natzweiler,
Dachau, Buchenwald, Auschwitz —
                                   Villages,
Pasture-bordered hamlets on the far side of the river.

8

The promise was broken too freely
To them and to their fathers, for them to care.
They survive like cedars on a cliff, roots
Hooked in any crevice they can find.
They walk Avenue C in shadows
Neither conciliating its Baalim
Nor whoring after landscapes of the senses,
Tarig bab el Amoud being in the blood
Fumigated by Puerto Rican cooking.

Among women girthed like cedar trees
Other, slender ones appear:
One yellow haired, in August,
Under shooting stars on the lake, who
Believed in promises which broke by themselves —
In a German flower garden in the Bronx
The wedding of a child and a child, one flesh
Divided in the Adirondack spring —
One who found in the desert city of the West
The first happiness, and fled therefore —
And by a southern sea, in the pines, one loved
Until the mist rose blue in the trees
Around the spiderwebs that kept on shining,
Each day of the shortening summer.

And as rubbish burns
And the pushcarts are loaded
With fruits and vegetables and empty crates
And clank away on iron wheels over cobblestones,

And merchants infold their stores
And the carp ride motionlessly sleeplessly
In the dark tank in the fishmarket,
The figures withdraw into chambers overhead —
In the city of the mind, chambers built
Of care and necessity, where, hands lifted to the blinds,
They glimpse in mirrors backed with the blackness of the world
Awkward, cherished rooms containing the familiar selves.

9

Children set fires in ashbarrels,
Cats prowl the fires, scraps of fishes burn.

A child lay in the flames.
It was not the plan. Abraham
Stood in terror at the duplicity.
Isaac whom he loved lay in the flames.
The Lord turned away washing
His hands without soap and water
Like a common housefly.

The children laugh.
Isaac means *he laughs.*
Maybe the last instant,
The dying itself, *is* easier,
Easier anyway than the hike
From Pitt the blind gut
To the East River of Fishes,
Maybe it is as the poet said,
And the soul turns to thee
O vast and well-veiled Death
And the body gratefully nestles close to thee —

I think of Isaac reading Whitman in Chicago,
The week before he died, coming across

Such a passage and muttering, Oi!
What shit! And smiling, but not for you — I mean,

For *thee*, Sane and Sacred Death!

10

It was Gold's junkhouse, the one the clacking
Carts that little men pad after in harnesses
Picking up bedbugged mattresses, springs
The stubbornness has been loved out of,
Chairs felled by fat, lampshades lights have burned through,
Linoleum the geometry has been scuffed from,
Carriages a single woman's work has brought to wreck,
Would come to in the dusk and unload before,
That the whole neighborhood came out to see
Burning in the night, flames opening out like
Eyelashes from the windows, men firing the tears in,
Searchlights smashing against the brick,
The water blooming up the walls
Like pale trees, reaching into the darkness beyond.

Nobody mourned, nobody stood around in pajamas
And a borrowed coat steaming his nose in coffee.
It was only Gold's junkhouse.
                              But this evening
The neighborhood comes out again, everything
That may abide the fire was made to go through the fire
And it was made clean: a few twisted springs,
Charred mattresses (crawling still, naturally),
Perambulator skeletons, bicycles tied in knots —
In a great black pile at the junkhouse door,
Smelling of burnt rubber and hair. Rustwater
Hangs in icicles over the windows and door,
Like frozen piss aimed at trespassers,
Combed by wind, set overnight. Carriages we were babies in,
Springs that used to resist love, that gave in

And were thrown out like whores — the black
Irreducible heap, mausoleum of what we were —
It is cold suddenly, we feel chilled,
Nobody knows for sure what is left of him.

11

The fishmarket closed, the fishes gone into flesh.
The smelts draped on each other, fat with roe,
The marble cod hacked into chunks on the counter,
Butterfishes mouths still open, still trying to eat,
Porgies with receding jaws hinged apart
In a grimace of dejection, as if like cows
They had died under the sledgehammer, perches
In grass-green armor, spotted squeteagues
In the melting ice meek-faced and croaking no more,
Mud-eating mullets buried in crushed ice,
Tilefishes with scales like bits of chickenfat.
Spanish mackerels with buttercups on the flanks,
Pot-bellied pikes, two-tone flounders
After the long contortion of pushing both eyes
To the brown side that they might look up,
Lying brown side down, like a mass laying-on of hands,
Or the oath-taking of an army.

The only things alive are the carp
That drift in the black tank in the rear,
Kept living for the usual reason, that they have not died,
And perhaps because the last meal was garbage and they might
    begin smelling
On dying, before the customer got halfway home.
They nudge each other, to be netted,
The sweet flesh to be lifted thrashing into the air,
To be slugged, and then to keep on living
While they are opened on the counter.

Fishes do not die exactly, it is more
That they go out of themselves, the visible part

Remains the same, there is little pallor,
Only the cataracted eyes which have not shut ever
Must look through the mist which crazed Homer.

These are the vegetables of the deep,
The Sheol-flowers of darkness, swimmers
Of denser darknesses where the sun's rays bend for the last time
And in the sky there burns this shifty jellyfish
That degenerates and flashes and re-forms.

Fishes are nailed to the wood,
The big Jew stands like Christ, nailing them to the wood,
He scrapes the knife up the grain, the scales fly,
He unnails them, reverses them, nails them again,
Scrapes and the scales fly. He lops off the heads,
Shakes out the guts as if they did not belong in the first place,
And they are flesh for the first time in their lives.

Dear Frau —————:

    Your husband, —————, died in the Camp Hospital on —————.
May I express my sincere sympathy on your bereavement. ————— was
admitted to the Hospital on ————— with severe symptoms of exhaus-
tion, complaining of difficulties in breathing and pains in the chest.
Despite competent medication and devoted medical attention, it proved
impossible, unfortunately, to keep the patient alive. The deceased voiced
no final requests.

                              Camp Commandant, —————

On 5th Street Bunko Certified Embalmer Catholic
Leans in his doorway drawing on a Natural Bloom Cigar.
He looks up the street. Even the Puerto Ricans are Jews
And the Chinese Laundry closes on Saturday.

12

Next door, outside the pink-fronted Bodega Hispano —

(A crying: you imagine
Some baby in its crib, wailing
As if it could foresee everything.
The crying subsides: you imagine
A mother or father clasping
The damned creature in their arms.
It breaks out again,
This time in a hair-raising shriek — ah,
The alleycat, in a pleasant guise,
In the darkness outside, in the alley,
Wauling slowly in its blood.

Another, loftier shrieking
Drowns it out. It begins always
On the high note, over a clang of bells:
Hook & Ladder 11 with an explosion of mufflers
Crab-walking out of 5th Street,
Accelerating up the Avenue, siren
Sliding on the rounded distances
Returning fainter and fainter,
Like a bee looping away from where you lie in the grass.

The searchlights catch him at the topfloor window,
Trying to move, nailed in place by the shine.

The bells of Saint Brigid's
On Tompkins Square
Toll for someone who has died —
J'oïs la cloche de Serbonne,
Qui toujours à neuf heures sonne
Le Salut que l'Ange prédit . . .

Expecting the visitation
You lie back on your bed,

The sounds outside
Must be outside. Here
Are only the dead spirituals
Turning back into prayers —
You rise on an elbow
To make sure they come from outside,
You hear nothing, you lay down
Your head on the pillow
Like a pick-up arm —
    swing low
           swing low
                    sweet
   lowsweet —)

— Carols of the Caribbean, plinkings of guitars.

13

The garbage disposal truck
Like a huge hunched animal
That sucks in garbage in the place
Where other animals evacuate it
Whines, as the cylinder in the rear
Threshes up the trash and garbage,
Where two men in rubber suits
(It must be raining outside)
Heap it in. The groaning motor
Rises in a whine as it grinds in
The garbage, and between-times
Groans. It whines and groans again.
All about it as it moves down
5th Street is the clatter of trashcans,
The crashes of them as the sanitary engineers
Bounce them on the sidewalk.

If it is raining outside
You can only tell by looking
In puddles, under the lifted streetlamps.

It would be the spring rain.

14

Behind the Power Station on 14th, the held breath
Of light, as God is a held breath, withheld,
Spreads the East River, into which fishes leak:
The brown sink or dissolve,
The white float out in shoals and armadas,
Even the gulls pass them up, pale
Bloated socks of riverwater and rotted seed,
That swirl on the tide, punched back
To the Hell Gate narrows, and on the ebb
Steam seaward, seeding the sea.

On the Avenue, through air tinted crimson
By neon over the bars, the rain is falling.
You stood once on Houston, among panhandlers and winos
Who weave the eastern ranges, learning to be free,
To not care, to be knocked flat and to get up clear-headed
Spitting the curses out. "Now be nice,"
The proprietor threatens; "Be nice," he cajoles.
"Fuck you," the bum shouts as he is hoisted again,
"God fuck your mother." (In the empty doorway,
Hunched on the empty crate, the crone gives no sign.)

That night a wildcat cab whined crosstown on 7th.
You knew even the traffic lights were made by God,
The red splashes growing dimmer the farther away
You looked, and away up at 14th, a few green stars;
And without sequence, and nearly all at once,
The red lights blinked into green,
And just before there was one complete Avenue of green,
The little green stars in the distance blinked.

It is night, and raining. You look down
Towards Houston in the rain, the living streets,

Where instants of transcendence
Drift in oceans of loathing and fear, like lanternfishes,
Or phosphorus flashings in the sea, or the feverish light
Skin is said to give off when the swimmer drowns at night.

From the blind gut Pitt to the East River of Fishes
The Avenue cobbles a swath through the discolored air,
A roadway of refuse from the teeming shores and ghettos
And the Caribbean Paradise, into the new ghetto and new paradise,
This God-forsaken Avenue bearing the initial of Christ
Through the haste and carelessness of the ages,
The sea standing in heaps, which keeps on collapsing,
Where the drowned suffer a C-change,
And remain the common poor.

Since Providence, for the realization of some unknown purpose, has seen
fit to leave this dangerous people on the face of the earth, and did not
destroy it . . .

Listen! the swish of the blood,
The sirens down the bloodpaths of the night,
Bone tapping on the bone, nerve-nets
Singing under the breath of sleep —

We scattered over the lonely seaways,
Over the lonely deserts did we run,
In dark lanes and alleys we did hide ourselves . . .

The heart beats without windows in its night,
The lungs put out the light of the world as they
Heave and collapse, the brain turns and rattles
In its own black axlegrease —

                    In the nighttime
Of the blood they are laughing and saying,
Our little lane, what a kingdom it was!

                    oi weih, oi weih

Flower Herding on Mount Monadnock

PART I

The River That Is East

1

Buoys begin clanging like churches
And peter out. Sunk to the gunwhales
In their shapes tugs push upstream.
A carfloat booms down, sweeping past
Illusory suns that blaze in puddles
On the shores where it rained, past the Navy Yard,
Under the Williamsburg Bridge
That hangs facedown from its strings
Over which the Jamaica Local crawls,
Through white-winged gulls which shriek
And flap from the water and sideslip in
Over the chaos of illusions, dangling
Limp red hands, and screaming as they touch.

2

A boy swings his legs from the pier,
His days go by, tugs and carfloats go by,
Each prow pushing a whitecap. On his deathbed
Kane remembered the abrupt, missed Grail
Called Rosebud, Gatsby must have thought back
On his days digging clams in Little Girl Bay
In Minnesota, Nick fished in dreamy Michigan,
Gant had his memories, Griffiths, those
Who went baying after the immaterial
And whiffed its strange dazzle in a blonde
In a canary convertible, who died
Thinking of the Huck Finns of themselves

On the old afternoons, themselves like this boy
Swinging his legs, who sees the *Ile de France*
Come in, and wonders if in some stateroom
There is not a sick-hearted heiress sitting
Drink in hand, saying to herself his name.

3

A man stands on the pier.
He has long since stopped wishing his heart were full
Or his life dear to him.
He watches the snowfall hitting the dirty water.
He thinks: Beautiful. Beautiful.
If I were a gull I would be one with white wings,
I would fly out over the water, explode, and
Be beautiful snow hitting the dirty water.

4

And thou, River of Tomorrow, flowing . . .
We stand on the shore, which is mist beneath us,
And regard the onflowing river. Sometimes
It seems the river stops and the shore
Flows into the past. Nevertheless, its leaked promises
Hopping in the bloodstream, we strain for the future,
Sometimes even glimpse it, a vague, scummed thing
We dare not recognize, and peer again
At the cabled shroud out of which it came,
We who have no roots but the shifts of our pain,
No flowering but our own strange lives.

What is this river but the one
Which drags the things we love,
Processions of debris like floating lamps,
Towards the radiance in which they go out?

No, it is the River that is East, known once
From a high window in Brooklyn, in agony — river
On which a door locked to the water floats,
A window sash paned with brown water, a whisky crate,
Barrel staves, sun spokes, feathers of the birds,
A breadcrust, a rat, spittle, butts, and peels,
The immaculate stream, heavy, and swinging home again.

The Homecoming of Emma Lazarus

1

Having no father anymore, having got up
In England without hope, having sailed the strewn
Atlantic and been driven under Bedloe
In the night, where the Green Lady lifts
Over that slow, bleating, most tragic of harbors,

Her burning hand, Emma came floating home,
To the thick, empty whistling of the tugs.
Thoreau's pocket compass had been her keepsake,
She made her way in without it, through the fog,
It was hard for her, in fact, coming in to die,

A little unfair, her father having died already.
In the attic on Union Square? Thrown out? Ah,
Somewhere in the mess of things! From Governor's Island
A bugler's loneliest notes roll slowly in,
And birds rock in the fog on the slapping waves.

2

As a child she had chased a butterfly
Through Battery Park, the only one decorating
Manhattan that afternoon, its clumsy, wind-thin
Wings making cathedral windows in the sun,

While the despised grandmother
With the gleety leashes, cruddy with age,
Of the eyebeams, held on. Alas, the crone's
Doughy ears must also have been golden in the sun!

It was towards you, gilded in the day's going down,
Green Lady, that we crawled — but from what ground of
    nausea
Had we turned, what relinquished plot of earth
Had we spit at, which was, anyway, the earth?

3

Dark haired, ephebic Emma, she knew
The night she floated into New York Harbor
Atlantis had sunk while she was abroad,
She could see the rainbows of it shining queerly
The many thousand leagues of her life away —

Weekends on Union Square, from his shaving mug
She blew bubbles crawling with colors that buoyed
Into the sunshine, she made up little rhymes,
She skipped rope, at her father's knee he put
Lilacs in her hair. Everybody loved her!

And on the last ride across 14th,
Did the English success suddenly become nothing,
Did the American childhood, including its odd affliction,
A neurotic longing to be English, turn out
To be the paradise she died longing for?

4

Facing the Old World the Green Lady whispers, "Eden!"
Seeing her looking so trim in American verdigris
They thought she was saying how it was here,
Seeing her looking to sea we heard the pure nostalgia,
Vacuumed in the wind from the Dry Cleaning Store
She may, herself, have wondered what she meant.

She crouches on the floor. She read once,
In the paper, a poem she had composed herself.

Was it just poetry, all that? It was pretty,
There is nothing she can do about it, it really was.
Her arm lies along the bench, her hand
Hangs over the edge as if she has just let something drop.

She has wept a long time now, and now poetry
Can do no more to her. Her shoulder shrugs as though
To drive away birds which, anyway, weren't intending
To alight. In the Harbor the conscript bugler
Blows the old vow of acceptance into the night —
It fades, and the wounds of all we had accepted open.

Old Arrivals

Molded in verdigris
Shortly before she died
The Lady stands by herself
Her electrical hand on fire.

They too in the Harbor
That chops the light to pieces
Looked up at her hand, burning,
Hair, flesh, blood, bone.

They floated in at night
On black water, cargoes
Which may not go back, waves
Breaking the rocks they break on.

Hunger unto Death

Her underarms
Clean as washbasins,
Her folds of fat resting
On layers of talcum-powdered flesh,
She proceeds towards cream-cheese-on-white,
Jelly pie, gum brownies, chocolate bars,
Rinsed down by tumblers of fresh milk,

Past the Trinity Graveyard
Filled with green, creepy plants,
Shiny-necked birds waddling about,
Monuments three-humped like children playing ghost,
Blackstone slabs racked with dates and elegies,

At which,
In the dark of the wide skirt,
First left then right,
Like a political campaigner pulling out of a station,
Her heavy rear rolls out its half-smiles of farewell,

While the face wheezes for grub,
And sweat skips and splashes from hummock down to
        hummock,
And inconceivable love clasps the fat of life to its pain.

Calcutta Visits

Overhead the fan wobbles on its axle.
In Delhi, on Gandhi's tomb, it said *Hai Ram* ("an old cry").
On Sudden Street they cry, "Hey Johnny,
Nice girl? Chinese, Indian, European, Mixed?"
She taps a fat foot, finicks with phonograph needles,
Fools with buttons. "No like dance,"
She announces, collapsing on the carpet, "Fookey!"
The bird will leave this branch at dawn
And fly away. For one full day remember her.

From this blue window? this blue, zigzagging street?
(*"Five? Five* already? Ah, den, come morning . . .")
A man in white skids towards your knees,
"A morsel! A morsel!" The only city
In the world where the beggars have read Dickens,
Says the Oxford Indian of his first homecoming,
As he sits up there in the Grand Hotel,
Among bribed, sleepy bellhops, drinking himself blind,
While the fan prowls the ceiling as in a zoo.

Floodtime. Cabs practically floating through town.
The driver sizes me up in the rearview mirror
With black, mystical eyes: how exactly to soak me . . .
A Bengal poet, disciple of Tagore,
His tongue flickering through his talk like a serpent's,
Looks from his window on the city. He says
Each day he has to transcend its pain anew.
His face darkens by the window and gives nothing away.
It is his pain, by the love that asks no way out.

Doppelgänger

1

I have to bribe the policeman
To keep him from arresting the driver
For trying to make me overpay him, which I've just done.

A sailor staggers up,
All his money blown on thieves he cries,
I pay him and he goes off hunting more thieves.

The fan whips up the heat,
The ice turns to slush
Before you can throw it into your whisky.

2

I remember at daybreak,
The air on the point of cooling
Was just starting to heat up,

I heard a voice in the distance,
I looked up, far away,
There at the beginning of the world

I could make out a beggar,
Down the long street he was calling *Galway!*
I started towards him and began calling *Galway!*

To a Child in Calcutta

Dark child in my arms, eyes
The whites of them just like mine
Gazing with black, shined canniness
At mine like large agates in a billboard,

Whom I held as a passerby
A few stricken days down Bandook Gulli,
While they were singing, upstairs,
Everyone in Calcutta is knocking at my door,

You are my conqueror! and you were
Calmly taking in my colored eyes and
Skin burned and thin and
Browned hardly at all by your Bengal sun:

If they show you, when you reach my age,
The blown-up snapshot they took of the stranger
Holding all you once were in his arms,
What will you be able to think, then,

Of the one who came from some elsewhere
And took you in his arms
And let you know the touch of a father
And the old warmth in a paw from nowhere,

But that in his nowhere
He will be dying, letting go his hold
On all for which his heart tore itself
As when they snapped you in his arms like his child,

And going by the photograph
That there was this man, his hair in his eyes,
His hand bigger than your whole head,
Who held you when helplessly

You let him, that between him and you
Were this gesture and this allowance
And he is your stranger father
And he dies in a strange land, which is his own.

In Calcutta, I thought,
Every pimp, taxidriver, whore, and beggar,
Dowsed for me through the alleys day and night —
In Bandook Gulli I came upon you,

On a street crossed by fading songs
I held you in my arms
Until you slept, in these arms,
In rags, in the pain of a little flesh.

Kyoto Prints

1

In the green air
Of before the dawn
The gutturals of the prayer
Pile up on formal hiccups.

2

The lake
Every point on whose shore
Keeps out of sight of some other point
Is drawn from the kokorai,
A character drawn from the heart.
In it is a flaw called the Pure Land.

3

A phallic,
Thousand-year gravestone rises,
Miko pick their way past
With chalk faces, on big shoes,
Pucka pucka pucka pucka

4

After the Ceremony of Kō
The girl draws out the coals
And pokes nine vents in the clay
To let out the old fire smell.

5

Tied to a few leaves
Attached loosely to the air
In the garden of moss and pine
An old eye with a spider in it
No longer troubles to look out,
A common disease of the eye
(With a pretty name:
I-Saw-the-Ghost-of-a-Flower . . .)

Koisimi Buddhist of Altitudes

He sees a skinny waterfall hanging
Like a bare root, a shape seeking water
Down which the particles of water crawl,
And climbs, crawling up the shined
Rock rubbing his fingerprints off,
And looks from the top at the land,
As it was, clawed from within, perfectly
Unbroken. He cries, *it is me,*
At the glare, and waits, and he hears
On the horizon the thin whine of wind
Machining its way to where he waits.
The first eddies begin picking up speed,
Sunlight and rock start circling
Around him, now they lose hold, and skid
Some degrees, appear to recover,
And now skid all the way out, and vanish.
What is this wind? Koisimi challenges.
It is not me, he knows, and leans
In any direction, which is the way.

Last Spring

Through a dark winter
In a cold chambre de bonne
I lay still and dreamed

And as we lose our grip
On the things of the world
Settling for their glitter

It was of the things
Whose corpses outlive them,
Shellfishes, ostriches, elephants.

2

But in spring the sun's
Swath of reality started going over
The room daily, like a cleaning woman,

It sent up my keepsakes,
My inventions in dust,
It left me only my solitude

And time to walk
Head bobbing out front like a pigeon's
Knocking on the instants to let me in.

Room of Return

Room over the Hudson
Where a naked light bulb
Lights coat hangers, whisky bottles,
Umbrellas, anti-war tracts, poems,
A potted plant trimmed to a crucifixion,

From which, out the front window,
You sometimes see
The *Vulcania* or the *France*
Or a fat *Queen*
Steaming through the buildings across the street,

To which every night
The alleycat sneaks up
To slop his saucer
Of fresh cream on the fire escape,
Washing down his rat,

Room crossed by wind from
Air conditioners' back ends,
By the clicking at all hours of invisible looms,
By cries of the night-market, hoofbeats, horns,
By bleats of boats also lost on the Hudson,

Room, anyway,
Where I switch the light on,
Tiny glimmer
Again, in this city
Pricking the sky, after an absence of years.

For Denise Levertov

Denise when you recited
With your intense unmusical voice
Poems on the objects of faith,
Buildings, rocks, birds, oranges,
A bum stood outside on Bleecker
Looking in through the glass
At you sitting in your green robe
Amid the Old World longhand
Of your utter, gently uttered
Solitude. Had you glanced up,
And had you seen his liquored eye,
The mowed cornfield of his gawk,
Maybe suddenly you would have seen
Him eye to eye, and paused,
And then gone on, in a room
Of cigarette smoke and coffee smells
And faithful friends, the hapless
Witness crying again in your breast.

Under the Williamsburg Bridge

1

I broke bread
At the riverbank,
I saw the black gull
Fly back black and crossed
By the decaying Paragon sign in Queens,
Over ripped water, it screamed
Killing the ceremony of the dove,
I cried those wing muscles
Tearing for life at my bones.

2

Tomorrow,
There on the Bridge,
Up in some riveted cranny in the sky,
It is true, the great and wondrous sun will be shining
On an old spider wrapping a fly in spittle-strings.

For Robert Frost

Why do you talk so much
Robert Frost? One day
I drove up to Ripton to ask,

I stayed the whole day
And never got the chance
To put the question.

I drove off at dusk
Worn out and aching
In my ears. Robert Frost,

Were you shy as a boy?
Do you go on making up
For some long period of solitude?

Is it simply that talk
Doesn't have to be metered and rhymed?
Or is talk distracting from something worse?

2

I saw you once on the TV,
Unsteady at the lectern,
The flimsy white leaf
Of hair standing straight up
In the wind, among top hats,
Old farmer and son

Of worse winters than this,
Stopped in the first dazzle

Of the District of Columbia,
Suddenly having to pay
For the cheap onionskin,
The worn-out ribbon, the eyes
Wrecked from writing poems
For us — stopped,
Lonely before millions,
The paper jumping in your grip,

And as the Presidents
Also on the platform
Began flashing nervously
Their Presidential smiles
For the harmless old guy,
And poets watching on the TV
Started thinking, Well that's
The end of *that* tradition,

And the managers of the event
Said, Boys this is it,
This sonofabitch poet
Is gonna croak,
Putting the paper aside
You drew forth
From your great faithful heart
The poem.

3

Once, walking in winter in Vermont,
In the snow, I followed a set of footprints
That aimed for the woods. At the verge
I could make out, "far in the pillared dark,"
An old creature in a huge, clumsy overcoat,

Lifting his great boots through the drifts,
Going as if to die among "those dark trees"
Of his own country. I watched him go,

Past a house, quiet, warm and light,
A farm, a countryside, a woodpile in its slow
Smokeless burning, alder swamps ghastly white,
Tumultuous snows, blanker whitenesses,
Into the pathless wood, one eye weeping,
The dark trees, for which no saying is dark enough,
Which mask the gloom and lead on into it,
The bare, the withered, the deserted.

There were no more cottages.
Soft bombs of dust falling from the boughs,
The sun shining no warmer than the moon,
He had outwalked the farthest city light,
And there, clinging to the perfect trees,
A last leaf. What was it?
What was that whiteness? — white, uncertain —
The night too dark to know.

4

He turned. *Love,*
Love of things, duty, he said,
And made his way back to the shelter
No longer sheltering him, the house
Where everything was turning to words,

Where he would think on the white wave,
Folded back, that rides in place on the obscure
Pouring of this life to the sea —
And seal the lips
Of his sorrow with the *mot juste.*

5

Poet of the country of white houses,
Of clearings going out to the dark wall of woods
Frayed along the skyline, you who nearly foreknew
The next lines of poems you suddenly dropped,
Who dwelt in access to that which other men
Have burnt all their lives to get near, who heard
The high wind, in gusts, seething
From far off, headed through the trees exactly
To this place where it must happen, who spent
Your life on the point of giving away your heart
To the dark trees, the dissolving woods,
Into which you go at last, heart in hand, deep in:
When we think of a man who was cursed
Neither with the mystical all-lovingness of Walt Whitman
Nor with Melville's anguish to know and to suffer,
And yet cursed . . . A man, what shall I say,
Vain, not fully convinced he was dying, whose calling
Was to set up in the wilderness of his country,
At whatever cost, a man, who would be his own man,
We think of you. And from the same doorway
At which you lived, between the house and the woods,
We see your old footprints going away across
The great Republic, Frost, up memorized slopes,
Down hills floating by heart on the bulldozed land.

PART II

Tillamook Journal (*2nd version*)

1

I have come here
From Chicago, packing
A sleeping bag, a pan
To melt snow for drinking,
Dried apricots, tea,
And a great boiled beef-
heart for gnawing on.

Two loggers drove me
As far in as they could get,
Two of the gunnysack loggers
Of the Burn, owning a truck
And a dozer, a few cables
And saws, who drag out
The sound heartwood for money.

They turned around
Where a rockslide had dumped itself,
One of them got out
And reached in the erosion
And showed me a handful
Of earth, more black
Ashes than it was earth.

2

A few years back,
They said, there'd

Been a prospector here,
An old man past seventy
Who believed the land,
Being otherwise worthless,
Ought to yield precious metal.

They would run across him,
A little, swaying heap of gear
Traipsing along
A logging road, or thrashing up
Some avalanching gravel, or
Mumbling about metal while staggering
Out of a vegetable gulley.

A full year
He hunted uranium or gold,
The Geiger counter lashed on
Like an extra heart,
Around January he'd have
Settled for anything at all,
When spring came he vanished.

3

I set out walking
From where they turned,
Underfoot the terrain spews
Rock and gravel,
Every step rattles and gives way,
Gigantic treetrunks
Barricade all the directions.

I wondered that a man
Of seventy-odd years had been able
To put up with one of them
On this breast, the ear

Pressed to the metal heart hearing
Only his own bloodbeat
And that getting fainter.

As the hill grew steep,
Up to my ankles in gravel
And grappling at roots and rocks
I traversed and wound along,
At last I came climbing up
On my hands and knees
As though I'd come here begging.

4

From the top of Cedar Butte
The whole compass is visible,
To the west the Pacific
Lies out flat and shiny,
Everywhere else are
Nothing but hills
Plunging across a saw-toothed country.

I looked back south
Where the hills have been logged off,
Except for a few clumps of snags
Out of reach
Or too burnt
Or decayed for profit
It is a total shambles,

White stumps,
White logs washing
To the valleys, bleeding scarps,
Lopped spurs, empty streambeds,
The whole land split and cracked
Under the crisscross of roads
And oozing down its ravines.

5

It is twenty-five years
Since the first blue-white puff
Kited up the wind,
The Douglas fir is potent only in fits,
An intolerant tree,
It breeds best in the open,
As in the aftermath of fire.

Convicts have put saplings
By the coast, schoolboys
Have planted by the highway,
Rain and sun continue falling,
Nothing catches,
A little fireweed, vine maple, grape,
Ants, black spiders . . .

To the north
On hills the loggers can't reach
The great virgin stands
Of snags
Burnt clean and bleached
In the distance keep on
Blurring into smoke.

6

All day the big,
Immaculate snowflakes
Have been coming down, melting
On touching. All night,
Wet through, trying for sleep,
I listened to Kilchis
River grinding its rocks and boulders.

The ravine is a mass
Of slash slippery

With rain and snow. Uprooted
Trees cross and lock each other
Blocking the water,
Tan, beautifully
Grained rims for the waterfalls.

At last a little
Mule deer joined me,
Leading like a scout,
When I turned off and climbed
He stopped too, and sadly,
It almost seemed, watched my going.
Some birds began wrangling and chirping.

7

At the sound of surf
I scramble to my feet
And climb again — from where I sat
Under the last knoll,
Gnawing the heart,
Looking back at the Burn
As it went out in the twilight,

Its crags broken,
Its valleys soaked in night,
Just one more of the
Plundered breasts of the world —
And hearing my heart
Beat in the air
I come over the last summit

Into a dark wind
Blasting out of the darkness,
Where before me the tempestuous ocean
Falls with long triple crashes on the shore

And where behind the snow is putting down
A last, saprophytic blossoming.
It is only steps to the unburnable sea.

On Hardscrabble Mountain

1

On old slashed spruce boughs
Buoying me up off the snow
I stretched out on the mountain,
Now and then a bit of snow
Would slide quietly from a branch,

Once a last deerfly came by,

I could see off for about a hundred miles.

2

I waked with a start,
The sun had crawled off me,
I was shivering in thick blue shadows,
Sap had stuck me to the spruce boughs.

The wind again starting to rise.

3

On the way down, passing
The little graveyard in the woods,
I gave a thought to the old skulls and bones lying there,

And I started praying to a bear just shutting his eyes,
To a skunk dozing off,

To a marmot with yellow belly,
To a dog-faced hedgehog,
To a dormouse with a paunch and large ears like leaves or wings.

On Frozen Fields

1

We walk across the snow,
The stars can be faint,
The moon can be eating itself out,
There can be meteors flaring to death on earth,
The Northern Lights can be blooming and seething
And tearing themselves apart all night,
We walk arm in arm, and we are happy.

2

You in whose ultimate madness we live,
You flinging yourself out into the emptiness,
You — like us — great an instant,

O only universe we know, forgive us.

In Fields of Summer

The sun rises,
The goldenrod blooms,
My own life is adrift in my body,
In my heart and hands, in my teeth,
It shines up at the old crane
Who holds out his drainpipe of a neck
And creaks along in the blue,

And the goldenrod shines with its life, too,
And the grass,
And the great field wavers and flakes,
The rumble of bumblebees keeps deepening,
A phoebe flutters up,
A lark bursts up all dew.

A Bird Comes Back

1

Only the head and the shoulders, only
The bust of a bird really,
Cochineal and emerald, appears
Stinging the blossoms, there
At the open window, amidst phlox,
Where there are, already,
Bees and three white butterflies,
His missing wings crackling deeply
As he needles the flowers.

2

The old timbers of the house
Shift sidewise, like stove grates,
One of the too-frequent settlings.
I think of Emily Dickinson's hummingbird.

3

Odd to see him now
With nothing in back of him
But New Hampshire fifty miles away and badly faded.

Cells Breathe in the Emptiness

1

The flowers turn to husks
And the great trees suddenly die
And rocks and old weasel bones lose
The little life they had
And the air quells and goes so still
It gives the ears something like the bends.

2

From the compost heap
Now arises the sound of the teeth
Of one of those sloppy green cabbageworms
Eating his route through a cabbage,
Now snarling like a petite chainsaw, now droning on . . .

A butterfly blooms on a buttercup,
From the junkpile flames up a junco.

Poem of Night

1

I move my hand over
Slopes, falls, lumps of sight,
Lashes barely able to be touched,
Lips that give way so easily
It's a shock to feel underneath them
The bones' smile.

Muffled a little, barely cloaked,
Zygoma, maxillary, turbinate.

2

I put my hand
On the side of your face,
You lean your head a little
Into my hand — and so,
I know you're a dormouse
Taken up in winter sleep,
A lonely, stunned weight.

3

A cheekbone,
A curved piece of brow,
A pale eyelid
Float in the dark,
And now I make out
An eye, dark,
Wormed with far-off, unaccountable lights.

4

Hardly touching, I hold
What I can only think of
As some deepest of memories in my arms,
Not mine, but as if the life in me
Were slowly remembering what it is.

You lie here now in your physicalness,
This beautiful degree of reality.

5

And now the day, raft that breaks up, comes on.

I think of a few bones
Floating on a river at night,
The starlight blowing in place on the water,
The river leaning like a wave towards the emptiness.

Nightfall of the Real

I. *House on the Cliff*

Swallows dart at one another
Across the curve of the moon. Two
Ravens tumble at the cliff and fall away. On the port
The orange, white, and blue umbrellas
Which have turned all day like sunflowers
Fold themselves. In the Bar des Guitares
They are raking the strings. It is evening.
Mullets are leaping in the straits.

II. *La Nappe Frugale*

On a table set by heart
In the last sun of the day
Olives, three fishes,
Bread, a bottle of *rosé.*

A rainbow crosses a fish,
A glass blossoms and reblossoms,
Flesh slides off bones which were,
We now see, only stabbing it.

Darkness sticks itself
To empty spines. Night climbs
In glasses. A breeze. Low
Voices. Paths floating on earth.

III. *Hour of the Lamp*

1

Olives, bread,
Fishes, pink wine:
Sudden in the dusk a
Crackling across stones.

To this table one came,
Came and ate, tore actual bread,
Felt physical drink touch his soul,
Here conversed, here laughed a last time.

2

Four faces looking in
On a vanished room — the vineyard,
The olive grove, the stones,
The green sea — begin vanishing.
In a room ready to turn white

A pause: out in the dark
The distant dull splash of a fish.
Yet again. Sick of weight
It leans up through its eerie life
Towards the night-flash of its emblemhood.

3

The spoon, the table, the mirrors,
The green portrait of a vase of flowers,
Each now streaks fatally with dusk.

The generating light goes out,
The rich time, which is twilight.
On the shore
A fern, fishy, and glittering.

Middle of the Way

1. I wake in the night,
   An old ache in the shoulder blades.
   I lie amazed under the trees
   That creak a little in the dark,
   The giant trees of the world.

   I lie on earth the way
   Flames lie in the woodpile,
   Or as an imprint, in sperm, of what is to be.
   I love the earth, and always
   In its darknesses I am a stranger.

2. 6 A.M. Water frozen again. Melted it and made tea. Ate a raw egg
   and the last orange. Refreshed by a long sleep. The trail practically
   indistinguishable under 8″ of snow. 9:30 A.M. Snow up to my
   knees in places. Sweat begins freezing under my shirt when I stop
   to rest. The woods are filled, anyway, with the windy noise of the
   first streams. 10:30 A.M. The sun at last. The snow starts to melt
   off the boughs at once, falling with little ticking sounds. Mist
   clouds are lying in the valleys. 11:45 A.M. Slow, glittering breakers
   roll in on the beaches ten miles away, very blue and calm. Odd to
   see it while sitting in snow. 12 noon. An inexplicable sense of joy,
   as if some happy news had been transmitted to me directly, by-
   passing the brain. 2 P.M. From the top of Gauldy I looked back
   into Hebo valley. Castle Rock sticks into a cloud. A cool breeze
   comes up from the valley, it is a fresh, earthly wind and tastes of
   snow and trees. It is not like those transcendental breezes that make
   the heart ache. It brings happiness. 2:30 P.M. Lost the trail. A
   woodpecker watches me wade about through the snow trying to

locate it. The sun has gone back of the trees. 3:10 P.M. Still hunting for the trail. Getting cold. From an elevation I have an open view to the SE, a world of timberless, white hills, rolling, weirdly wrinkled. Above them a pale half moon. 3:45 P.M. Going on by map and compass. I saw a deer a minute ago, he fled touching down every fifteen feet or so. 7:30 P.M. Made camp near the head of Alder Creek. Trampled a bed into the snow and filled it with boughs. Concocted a little fire in the darkness. Ate pork and beans. A slug or two of whisky burnt my throat. The night very clear. Very cold. That half moon is up there and a lot of stars have come out among the treetops. The fire has fallen to coals.

3. The coals go out,
   The last smoke weaves up
   Losing itself in the stars.
   This is my first night to lie
   In the uncreating dark.

   In the heart of a man
   There sleeps a green worm
   That has spun the heart about itself,
   And that shall dream itself black wings
   One day to break free into the beautiful black sky.

   I leave my eyes open,
   I lie here and forget our life,
   All I see is we float out
   Into the emptiness, among the great stars,
   On this little vessel without lights.

   I know that I love the day,
   The sun on the mountain, the Pacific
   Shiny and accomplishing itself in breakers,
   But I know I live half alive in the world,
   I know half my life belongs to the wild darkness.

Ruins under the Stars

I

All day under the turning
Swallows I have sat, beside ruins
Of a plank house sunk up to its windows
In burdock and raspberry canes,
The roof dropped, the foundation broken in,
Nothing left perfect but axe-marks on the beams.

A paper in a cupboard talks about "Mugwumps,"
In a V-letter a farmboy in the Marines has "tasted battle . . ."
The apples are pure acid on the tangle of boughs,
The pasture has gone to popple and bush.
Here on this perch of ruins
I listen for the crunch of the porcupines.

2

Overhead the skull-hill rises
Crossed on top by the stunted apple,
Infinitely beyond it, older than love or guilt,
Lie the stars ready to jump and sprinkle out of space.

Every night under those thousand lights
An owl dies, or a snake sloughs his skin,
A man looking up at night
Knows the homesickness of all things.

3

Sometimes I see them,
The south-going Canada geese,
At evening, coming down
In pink light, over the pond, in great,
Loose, always dissolving V's —
I go out into the field,
Amazed and moved, and listen
To the cold, lonely yelping
Of their tranced bodies in the sky.

4

This morning I watched
Milton Norway's sky-blue Ford
Dragging its ass down the dirt road
On the other side of the valley.

Later, off in the woods
A chainsaw was agonizing across the top of some stump.
A while ago the tracks of a little, snowy,
SAC bomber went crawling across heaven.

What of that little hairstreak
That was flopping and batting about
Deep in the goldenrod —
Did she not know, either, where she was going?

5

Just now I had a funny sensation,
As if some angel, or winged star,
Had been perched nearby.
In the chokecherry bush
There was a twig just ceasing to tremble . . .

The bats come in place of the swallows.
In the smoking heap of old antiques
The porcupine-crackle starts up again,
The bone-saw, the blood music of this sphere,
And up there the stars rustling and whispering.

Tree from Andalusia

1

This old bleached tree
Dumped on the Sagaponack beach . . .
The wind has lifted and only seethes
Far up among the invisible stars,
As once on Ferry Street, at night,
Among *to let* signs and closed wholesalers,
From some loft I heard a phrase of jazz,
y recuerdo una brisa triste por los olivos.

2

The wind starts fluting
In our teeth, in our ears,
It whines down the harmonica
Of the fingerbones, moans at the skull . . .

Blown on by their death
The things on earth whistle and cry out.

Spindrift

1

On this tree thrown up
From the sea, its tangle of roots
Letting the wind go through, I sit
Looking down the beach: old
Horseshoe crabs, broken skates,
Sand dollars, sea horses, as though
Only primeval creatures get destroyed,
At chunks of sea-mud still quivering,
At the light as it glints off the water
And the billion facets of the sand,
At the soft, mystical shine the wind
Blows over the dunes as they creep.

2

Sit down
By the clanking shore
Of this bitter, beloved sea,

Pluck sacred
Shells from the icy surf,
Fans of gold light, sunbursts,

Lift one to the sun
As a sign you accept to go,
All the way to the shrine of the dead.

3

This bleached root
Drifted from some foreign shore,
Brittle, cold, practically weightless, worn
Down to the lost grip it always essentially was,

If it has lost hold
It at least keeps the splayed
Shape of what it held,

And remains the hand
Of that gravel, one of earth's
Wandering icons of "to have."

4

I sit listening
To the surf as it falls,
The power and inexhaustible freshness of the sea,
The suck and inner boom
As a wave tears free and crashes back
In overlapping thunders going away down the beach.

It is the most we know of time,
And it is our undermusic of eternity.

5

I think of how I
Sat by a dying woman,
Her shell of a hand,
Wet and cold in both of mine,
Light, nearly out, existing as smoke,
I sat in the glow of her wan, absorbed smile.

6

Under the high wind
That moans in the grass
And whistles through crabs' claws
I sit holding this little lamp,
This icy fan of the sun.

Across gull tracks
And wind ripples in the sand
The wind seethes. My footprints
Slogging for the absolute
Already begin vanishing.

7

What does he really love,
That old man,
His wrinkled eyes
Tortured by smoke,
Walking in the ungodly
Rasp and cackle of old flesh?

The swan dips her head
And peers at the mystic
In-life of the sea,
The gull drifts up
And eddies towards heaven,
The breeze in his arms . . .

Nobody likes to die
But an old man
Can know
A kind of gratefulness
Towards time that kills him,
Everything he loved was made of it.

Flower Herding on Mount Monadnock

I

I can support it no longer.
Laughing ruefully at myself
For all I claim to have suffered
I get up. Damned nightmarer!

It is New Hampshire out here,
It is nearly the dawn.
The song of the whippoorwill stops
And the dimension of depth seizes everything.

2

The song of a peabody bird goes overhead
Like a needle pushed five times through the air,
It enters the leaves, and comes out little changed.

The air is so still
That as they go off through the trees
The love songs of birds do not get any fainter.

3

The last memory I have
Is of a flower which cannot be touched,

Through the bloom of which, all day,
Fly crazed, missing bees.

4

As I climb sweat gets up my nostrils,
For an instant I think I am at the sea,

One summer off Cap Ferrat we watched a black seagull
Straining for the dawn, we stood in the surf,

Grasshoppers splash up where I step,
The mountain laurel crashes at my thighs.

5

There is something joyous in the elegies
Of birds. They seem
Caught up in a formal delight,
Though the mourning dove whistles of despair.

But at last in the thousand elegies
The dead rise in our hearts,
On the brink of our happiness we stop
Like someone on a drunk starting to weep.

6

I kneel at a pool,
I look through my face
At the bacteria I think
I see crawling through the moss.

My face sees me,
The water stirs, the face,
Looking preoccupied,
Gets knocked from its bones.

7

I weighed eleven pounds
At birth, having stayed on
Two extra weeks in the womb.
Tempted by room and fresh air
I came out big as a policeman
Blue-faced, with narrow red eyes.
It was eight days before the doctor
Would scare my mother with me.

Turning and craning in the vines
I can make out through the leaves
The old, shimmering nothingness, the sky.

8

Green, scaly moosewoods ascend,
Tenants of the shaken paradise,

At every wind last night's rain
Comes splattering from the leaves,

It drops in flurries and lies there,
The footsteps of some running start.

9

From a rock
A waterfall,
A single trickle like a strand of wire,
Breaks into beads halfway down.

I know
The birds fly off
But the hug of the earth wraps
With moss their graves and the giant boulders.

10

In the forest I discover a flower.

The invisible life of the thing
Goes up in flames that are invisible
Like cellophane burning in the sunlight.

It burns up. Its drift is to be nothing.

In its covertness it has a way
Of uttering itself in place of itself,
Its blossoms claim to float in the Empyrean,

A wrathful presence on the blur of the ground.

The appeal to heaven breaks off.
The petals begin to fall, in self-forgiveness.
It is a flower. On this mountainside it is dying.